I0141946

The Donald Trump Syndrome

The Donald Trump Syndrome

WHY WOMEN CHOOSE THE WRONG MEN TO LOVE

Rich Gosse

Copyright 2017 Rich Gosse
All rights reserved.
ISBN-13: 9780934377188
ISBN-10: 0934377189
Library of Congress Control Number: 2017908957
Marin Publications, San Rafael, CA

Dedication

To The Seva Foundation, which has restored sight to millions of poor people worldwide.

All profits from this book will be donated to the foundation.

Make your own donation to The Seva Foundation, 1786 Fifth Street, Berkeley CA 94710, www.seva.org

Rich Gosse has been acclaimed by the news media:

"America's leading singles-ologist." *Sydney Morning Herald*

"The Sultan of Singledom." *The West Australian* and *The Sacramento Bee*

"The Date Doctor." *Associated Press*

"Mr. Single." *San Francisco Chronicle*

"The Singles Guru." *Las Vegas Review Journal*

"America's foremost authority on finding a romantic partner."
   National Singles Register

"The High Guru of Happy Singledom." *Oakland Tribune*

"The Billy Graham of the Singles World." *New Zealand Herald*

"Cupid's Proxy." *Long Beach Press Telegram*

"Mr. Single of California." *Riverside Press-Enterprise*

"A Walking Encyclopaedia on Luring the Opposite Sex." *New Zealand Herald*

"The Singles Evangelist." *Vallejo Times-Herald*

"The Singles Swami." *Tacoma News Tribune* and *San Francisco Examiner*

"The Love Guru." *Santa Barbara News-Press*

"The Dating Maven." *Hayward Daily Review*

"The Love Doctor." *Waukesha WI Freeman*

"America's foremost flirting authority." *New Zealand Herald on Sunday*

He lives up to them all.

Rich Gosse is the author of eight books on dating, including *You CAN Hurry Love*, *Singles Guide to America*, and *A Good Man Is EASY to Find* ("This is a great book!" Oprah Winfrey). His entertaining dating seminars have been sponsored by over 60 colleges. He is the chairman of The Society of Single Professionals, the world's largest non-profit singles organization; and Executive Director of The International Association of Dating Websites. His controversial views on dating have been featured by hundreds of major TV/Radio/Print media, including *Oprah*, NBC's *Today Show*, ABC's *Night Line*, Fox's *Neil Cavuto Show*, CNBC, MSNBC, BBC, *The London Times*, *The Australian*, *The New Zealand Herald*, *Newsweek*, *Cosmopolitan*, *Playboy*, *Playgirl*, etc. His personal website is RichGosse.com.

Table of Contents

PART 1
The Donald Trump Syndrome

Donald Trump lost the women's vote by twelve percentage points in the 2016 Presidential Election. But when it comes to marriage, he is clearly the lady's choice. Most single women over 40 would react with horror if they were told they desire a Donald Trump-like husband, but that's what many secretly want.

Donald Trump personifies many qualities that attract most women:

Older

For millennia women of all cultures have preferred older men. Despite all the stories of cougars dating younger men, women today are not much different. Women of all cultures, including that of America, have a strong preference for older men. The average American bachelorette marries a man at least two years older than she. Enter Donald Trump, age 71, the personification of the older, financially secure man who can easily attract women a half century younger than he.

This is despite the fact that older men are in short supply, particularly as women age. 1% more boy babies are born each year than girls. That extra percentage of men dies off quickly, so that by age 30 there is a 50-50 male-female ratio. From that point on, men start dropping off like flies. By age 60, for every bachelor in the U.S. there are three and a half single women. Yet despite these poor odds, most women still are looking for someone older.

Sociologists tell us that women prefer older men because they are more established in their careers and can therefore provide for a family. And menopausal women who no longer plan to bear children still cling to this ageist prejudice. Often they spurn young, attractive men in preference for their older counterparts. Or to be blunt, as men age, lose their hair, gain wrinkles, and develop pot bellies, they are more in demand than ever in the dating market. Conversely, young men with flat bellies, full manes of hair, and rippling muscles struggle to find a date. There is a 60% surplus of single men in America in their late 20s, so many make advances towards older women. Often in vain. Just as older men in general prefer younger women, older women are often prejudiced against younger men. This is the great paradox of dating in America.

Women who marry older men are tempting fate, since the average American woman outlives a man by five years. That's why two-thirds of nursing home residents are women. The antidote to widowhood is to marry a younger man.

Taller

God help single men who is short! The prejudice against them in the dating world is severe. That's why so many men claim to be over six feet tall in their online dating profiles, despite the fact that only 10% of American men have this distinction. "I want to be taller than my dance partner when I put on my heels," is the common refrain of single women.

Again we encounter Donald Trump, who at 6'3" tall literally stands out.

Wealthier

Most women object to being identified as being materialistic. "I don't care how much a man makes," they exclaim," so long as he has a good heart and loves me." Would that this were true! UNEMPLOYED is the #1 disqualifier in the dating world, if you are a man. No amount of wonderful qualities can overcome the obstacle of not having enough money. If you don't believe this, ask a woman if she would date a man looking for a job. As a multi-billionaire, again Donald Trump appears to be the ideal man to marry.

Historically women have been almost totally dependent on men financially. While today this is far less true in America, women in this country still earn only eight three cents on the dollar, in comparison to men. So income is rightfully a concern for many women.

Well-Educated

Newsweek magazine once claimed infamously that "College-educated women over 40 have a greater chance of being killed by terrorists than finding a husband." This outrageous claim was based on a "college-educated" woman limiting her choices to an older, better-educated, higher-income bachelor, since there is a severe shortage of such men. This was not always true. Until recent decades the vast majority of college graduates were men. Today most college graduates in America are WOMEN, as are most law school graduates. This is also true in many other fields. Women find that as they earn advanced degrees and higher incomes, they price themselves out of the marriage market. It becomes harder and harder for them to find older, better-educated, higher-income men than themselves who are available for marriage. This is particularly true for the African-American population, where the overwhelming percentage of well-educated high-income romantic eligibles are women.

Again Donald Trump appears as the ideal husband. As he so often reminds us, "I went to the finest schools."

Dominant Alpha Male

Most women are attracted to the Alpha Male, the leader of the pack. Many alpha males expect to date, seduce, and marry young, beautiful women. The Donald Trumps of the world feel entitled to not only attract the most desirable women in the world, but to be physically intimate with them almost immediately.

PART 2
The Ugly Side of Donald Trump

n Part One we saw Donald Trump as an older, taller, wealthier, better-educated, and dominant alpha male. Unfortunately Donald Trump also has many qualities that most women find abhorrent. Many men who are charismatic like Trump also share these negative qualities.

Womanizer

It's no secret that Donald Trump has cheated repeatedly on his three wives. Apparently that's not a disqualifier with many women. Mr. Trump had no problem seducing them, whether he or they were married or single.

A recent large study revealed that most women find married men to be more attractive than bachelors. The authors of the study speculated that this made sense, since married men have been pre-screened by their wives and found to be worthy of matrimony. Sadly, single men are not held in high esteem by many women. "All the best ones are taken." "There's got to be something wrong with him, otherwise he'd be married by now." "He is commitment phobic." While there may be some truth to these platitudes, they overgeneralize. Many men who would make good husbands have pursued an advanced degree or a challenging career rather than settle down. The cliché that "timing is everything" is no more true than in the case of choosing a man who finally is ready to settle down and pursue romantic goals. It would be wise to be sensitive to indicators that a man is too distracted to commit to one woman. But it would be equally important to be open to the possibility that a man has "sown his wild oats" and established himself in the world to the point that he is ready for the next stage of his life. All too often such men are dismissed out of hand.

Most women do not plan on marrying a womanizer who will cheat on them. Unfortunately, womanizers like Trump are often very smooth. They flatter a woman and may even buy her expensive gifts. Beware of men who appear to be too good to be true. They often are. And it's very easy for the Trumps of the world to stray, since they attract beautiful women almost effortlessly. There are millions of women, married and single, who see a married man as an intriguing challenge. A married man who is well-dressed, successful, and charming is irresistible to them. If you marry a Trump-like man, they will always be your rivals and try to steal your man.

Narcissistic

In the ancient Greek legend, Narcissus is a beautiful boy in love with himself who falls into a pool staring at his refection, and drowns. Donald Trump is the classic narcissist. The whole universe revolves around him and his needs. Narcissists feel entitled to everything they want. According to Ramani Durvasula, author of *Should I Go? Surviving a Relationship with a Narcissist*, they chronically seek admiration and validation. They tend to be superficial, greedy, and vain.

George Simon, a clinical psychologist who conducts seminars on manipulative behavior, says Trump is "so classic that I'm archiving video clips of him to use in workshops because there's no better example" of narcissism. "Otherwise I would have had to hire actors and write vignettes. He's like a dream come true." "Textbook narcissistic personality disorder," echoed clinical psychologist Ben Michaelis.

"He's very easy to diagnose," said psychotherapist Charlotte Prozan. "In the first debate, he talked over people and was domineering. He'll do anything to demean others, like tell Carly Fiorina he doesn't like her looks. 'You're fired!' would certainly come under lack of empathy. And he wants to deport immigrants, but [two of] his wives have been immigrants."

Gersh Kuntzman writes in *The New York Daily News* (January 29, 2017), that "The American Psychiatric Association says that anyone exhibiting five of the following nine egotistical traits has Narcissistic Personality Disorder." How many of these does President Trump exhibit? Mr. Kuntzman counts eight. You be the judge.

1. Grandiose sense of self-importance
2. Preoccupied with fantasies of unlimited success, power, brilliance, beauty, or ideal love.
3. Believes that he or she is "special" and unique and can only be understood by, or should associate with other special or high-status people.
4. Requires excessive admiration.
5. Has a sense of entitlement.
6. Is interpersonally exploitative.
7. Lacks empathy.
8. Is often envious of others or believes that others are envious of him or her.
9. Shows arrogant, haughty behaviors or attitudes

High self-esteem is a healthy psychological trait. But with Donald Trump, we see excessive self-love and grandiosity and a sense of entitlement. Romantic relationships with narcissists rarely are happy and fulfilling. Narcissists are too self-centered. They can't do the give and take that makes marriage work because everything is all about them.

Narcissists like Donald Trump have very little interest in a romantic partner's needs, feelings, or experiences. He is only interested in you supplying him with the attention, praise, and sex he requires.

Unfortunately narcissists can be very attractive to women. That's because they have worked extra hard to develop their charm and wit. They often become excellent salesmen, promoters, and political candidates because they feel the need to "sell themselves" to everyone. They have an obsessive need to be loved (or at least admired) by everyone. As a result, they often seduce women into not just sleeping with them, but into falling in love with them.

As long as you supply narcissists with what they need, including constant affirmation, they will stay with you. But if they perceive you turning against them, even in trivial ways, they can become angry and vengeful. President Trump's constant tirades on Twitter and during media interviews illustrate how spiteful a narcissist can be. You will always be on "needles and pins" with such a man, knowing at any moment he can explode and turn on you, whether you are his wife, business associate, or friend.

Women don't necessarily prefer narcissists. It's just who they notice, especially at social events. The less flashy men get little or no attention. As Donald Trump has proven, narcissistic men have no shortage of women who seek their company and dream of marital bliss with them. Personal Note: As a recovering narcissist myself, I understand this behavior. I didn't marry until late in life partially because I didn't have the interpersonal skills needed to create a healthy, loving, intimate relationship with a woman. It took many years of study (for example, at The Esalen Institute in Big Sur, California,) seminars, encounter groups, etc. for me to learn how to achieve intimacy. I'm happily married now for 17 years, but everyone who knew me earlier in my life thought I would never have a lasting relationship. I'm an example of someone who was capable of changing, but my narcissistic tendencies were tiny next to someone like Donald Trump. Men with an extreme level of narcissism are unlikely to ever change. So my most urgent advice to you if you encounter a narcissist in the dating jungle is to run for the hills! He will not change, not now, not ever.

Sociopathic Tendencies?

A sociopath is someone who has no conscience, who uses and abuses others without regret. While a sociopath can appear on the surface to be loving and caring, his interest in others stops when they are no longer of use to him.

According to *FoxNews.com* (June 10, 2016), "Donald Trump has been sued at least 60 times by individuals and businesses who accuse him of failing to pay for work done at his various properties, according to two published reports." Fox News goes on to mention that over 200 liens have been filed against Trump's companies by contractors or employees. *USA Today* published an expose on June 9, 2016 entitled "Hundreds allege Donald Trump doesn't pay his bills." The sub-headline read "Among Those Who Say

Billionaire Didn't Pay: Dishwashers, Painters, Waiters. The article goes on to say that "Trump's companies have also been cited for 24 violations of the Fair Labor Standards Act since 2005 for failing to pay overtime or minimum wage, according to U.S. Department of Labor data."

Reuters.com (Nov 13, 2015) writes that "the billionaire front-runner…says he sometimes refuses to pay bills from contractors he has hired and then forces them to negotiate the final figure down." Mr. Trump's strategy is to refuse to pay the full amount he owes them, and then challenge them to sue. In most cases they can't afford to sue, because the amount they would recover would not be enough to both make a profit and cover their legal fees.

Trump University is a good example of how Donald Trump exploits people, particularly the gullible. President Trump has agreed to pay $25 million to students who claimed he defrauded them. Of course as part of the legal settlement, he did not admit guilt. People with sociopathic tendencies never do. They do not have the capacity to feel guilty.

Donald Trump shocked many when he Frank Luntz of CNN asked him whether he has ever asked God for foregiveness for his actions. "I am not sure I have. I just go on and try to do a better job from there. I don't think so." A man with no conscience doesn't ever ask for forgiveness.

Accused Rapist

Ivana Trump, Trump's first wife, accused him, under oath, of raping her. Later she recanted. According to Mrs. Trump's original sworn testimony, Mr. Trump was livid at her after painful scalp reduction surgery, performed by her plastic surgeon, to remove a bald spot. "Your (expletive) doctor has ruined me!" said Mr. Trump, according to Harry Hurt III's 1993 book, *Lost Tycoon: The Many Lives of Donald J. Trump*. Mr. Hurt goes on to say that "Donald held back Ivana's arms and began to pull fistfuls of hair from her scalp. He tore off her clothes and unzipped his pants…"

Many people mistakenly believe that rape is a crime of passion. The truth is that rape is usually a crime of anger. And we know that Donald Trump is often a very angry man. His angry eruptions towards his employees and advisors is legendary. So Ivana's original testimony is very believable.

Twelve other women have accused President Trump of touching them inappropriately or other malign behaviors. Mr. Trump has denied all of these allegations, of course. You be the judge. Mr. Trump even admitted to what some regard as sexual battery in the famous sex tape with Billy Bush.

The irony is that Mr. Trump branded undocumented Mexican workers as rapists. Some people call this hypocrisy.

Groper and Voyeur

Mr. Trump had a disturbing habit of walking into changing rooms where teenage girls were dressing and undressing at his Miss Teen USA Contest. Tasha Dixon, Miss Teen Arizona, says Trump "just came strolling right in. There was no second to put a robe on or any sort of clothing or anything. Some girls were topless. Others were naked." Trump did the same at his Miss Universe Contest, according to Ms. Dixon. "To have the owner come waltzing in, when we're naked, or half-naked, in a very physically vulnerable position..."

Lest you think that Ms. Dixon made this all up, Trump admitted to this gross behavior while being interviewed by Howard Stern. "I'll go backstage before a show, and everyone's getting dressed and ready and everything else," Trump said.

Braggart

Donald Trump's bravado conveys the image of a man of high self-esteem, but the opposite is true. His deep-down insecurity requires that he constantly reassure himself (and the world) that he is the greatest. Proof of his inner low self-esteem is his notorious thin skin, which results in his angrily lashing out at anyone who questions his supremacy. Like the ten year old on the playground, he develops silly names for his rivals or perceived enemies. Hillary Clinton becomes "Crooked Hillary"; Ted Cruz is "Lyin' Ted"; Bernie Sanders is "Crazy Bernie"; Jeb Bush is "Low-energy"; Marco Rubio is "Little Marco"; Elizabeth Warren is "Pocahontas," and so forth.

Most women rightly prefer a man with high self-esteem. But sadly they often conflate self-worth with braggadocio. They mistake bluster for true self-worth. A man with a healthy self-image doesn't need to tear people down and call them names. Nor does he make silly claims such as "I am smarter than the generals" or "My I.Q. is one of the highest."

Liar

Politicians are held in ill repute in our society. It's no secret that many are highly polished liars. But Donald Trump takes lying to new levels beyond anything we've ever seen in modern American political history.

PolitiFact, which is non-partisan, found that 70 percent of the statements by Trump which they checked were lies. Only 15 percent were completely or mostly true. In contrast, "crooked Hillary" lied 26 percent of the time. See the Appendix at the end of this book for a list of Mr. Trump's most egregious lies.

Often Trump retweets lies, so that he personally cannot be accused of being a liar. In effect he is saying, "Hey, I'm just letting you know what other people think. I don't necessarily agree with them." For example, 3 times he retweeted claims that President Obama had released a false birth certificate. Let's be clear that if you quote a liar in a retweet, you are also lying!

Most people are basically honest and assume that others are like them. They are vulnerable to a World Champion Prevaricator like Donald Trump, who sweet talked them into voting for him to the supreme position of power on the planet. Trump-like bachelors can be equally adept at telling a woman what she wants to hear: "I love you," "I will always be faithful," "You're beautiful." Don't be a victim. Someone who plays fast and loose with the truth is not someone to be trusted with your happiness.

Don't Be Duped

How did Donald Trump, a man with no government experience, very little knowledge of international affairs, and an immature psyche persuade America to place into his hands the nuclear codes? He was lucky to have an opponent who was supremely qualified to be President in terms of experience (First Lady, United States Senator, Secretary of State) but had no charisma.

In the dating arena similar tragic choices are routine. 3 beautiful women (Ivana, Marla, and Melania Trump) chose to not only date but to marry Donald Trump. It wasn't just that he was older, taller, wealthier, and better-educated than most men. He was also more charismatic. Likewise millions of single women allow themselves to be seduced by flawed men who present a flashy package, rather than go with less flamboyant men of substance who don't know how to manipulate souls to their advantage. The rest of this book is dedicated to helping you identify the right man for a healthy, loving relationship and revealing where and how to meet him. Here's a hint: he will be the diametric opposite of Donald Trump!

PART 3
Redefining Mr. Right

f you have a single daughter, would you want her to marry a Donald Trump clone? Probably not. And yet mothers still tell their daughters that "it's just as easy to love a rich man as it is to love a poor one." The first thing most mothers ask a daughter after she meets a new man is not "Is he a good man? Is He loving? Is he faithful?" No, instead she asks "What does he do?" Even though most people claim they don't believe money is the key to happiness, the fact is that in America the dollar is king. Subconsciously, if not consciously, most Americans prioritize the search for wealth on the road to happiness. And if you can't earn it yourself or inherit it, the surest path to financial security is to find someone wealthy to marry. That explains the popularity of websites such as *SugarDaddyForMe.com* and *Seeking Arrangement.com*.

Sadly, the average bachelorette in America consciously or unconsciously craves a husband with many of Donald Trump's qualities. This is despite the fact that their chances of getting a man like Trump to marry them are slim or none. President Trump is not currently on the marriage market, but should he ever find himself in search of Wife Number Four, she will be young, slim, and beautiful, and most likely amply endowed. You can bet the house on that one. There are literally tens of millions of single women in America who are hoping to attract the older, taller, wealthier, better-educated, dominant man, who always has a beautiful woman on his arm, even though the competition for these alpha males is just too tough. Only the tiniest percentage of women in America will achieve this goal.

Meanwhile, millions of bachelors who might make excellent husbands are passed over. They spend most Saturday nights at home on their computers fantasizing about beautiful women, who never give them a second thought. These men are too young, short, poor, less educated, nice, unpretentious, and shy to attract a second glance.

Most women will tell you that a good man is hard to find and that all the good ones are already taken. This is TRUE, if you define a good man as being older, taller, wealthier, better-educated, narcissistic, dominant, and a womanizer. But if women overcome *The Donald Trump Syndrome*, they will discover that there is absolutely no shortage of men who would make excellent husbands. And the best part is that THERE IS NO COMPETITION FOR THESE GOOD MEN. Males who lack Mr. Trump's qualities are invisible in the dating world. Ironically, while so many millions of single women in America are competing for Trump-like men who are in such short supply, there is a cornucopia of good men available. Personal Note: I live in the San Francisco Bay Area, where women at my dating seminars and singles parties lament that all the good men are "married, gay, or dead." This is despite the fact that even when you subtract the 24% of single men who are gay in San Francisco, there still are a vast number of straight bachelors. 40 miles down the highway in San Jose, the straight bachelors are even more plentiful. San Jose is the only major city in America that has a surplus of bachelors. And these men tend to be intelligent, well-educated, and high earners. While the numbers are not as good elsewhere in America, there are still many millions of available bachelors. All you have to do to find them is to redefine what you consider to be a good man.

Reviewing Past Relationships

Philosopher George Santayana once said, "Those who do not remember the past are condemned to repeat it". So before defining a good man, review your past relationships to see if there is a pattern. Do you find that you re attracted to a certain "type" of man with fatal flaws? For example, do you find womanizers like Donald Trump to be irresistible? Are you drawn consistently to men with substance abuse problems (alcohol or drugs)? Do you find men who need "fixing" to be irresistible?

Some women go beyond being attracted to toxic men—they become addicted. They allow these men to treat them shabbily. They find themselves constantly defending their guy, even though all of their relatives and friends hate him. Shannon Colleary writes in *The Huffington Post* that the first step in Addiction Recovery is "admitting to yourself that you have a problem." The next step is to "decide to quit," followed by "writing a list of important reasons to quit your addiction, making a plan to quit, setting a concrete date to quit, seeking personal and professional support, identifying your triggers, and then actually quitting and handling withdrawal." You may wish to read *Toxic Men: 10 Ways to Identify, Deal With, and Heal From the Men Who Make Your Life Miserable*, by Dr. Lillian Glass.

Don't move on to a new relationship if your romantic past has been one disaster after another. Deal with your addiction to toxic men, then move on to someone with whom you can have a healthy relationship.

Defining a Good Man

If you don't know where you're going, you are unlikely to arrive at your destination. So the first step is to define a good man. Goal-setting experts all agree that it's critical to write down your goals, not keep them in your head. Writing them down makes them more concrete and real. And they are a constant reminder of what you seek. So before leaving the comfort of your home in search of Mr. Right, create a *Wish List* of all the traits you seek in a romantic partner. Make this list as complete and specific as possible. Everyone says they want to meet someone honest, but on a scale of 1 to 10, how honest do you want him to be? Do you want a 10, someone who tells you EVERYTHING, no matter how much it hurts your feelings? Or, like most people, would you prefer a 5? Someone who tells you the nice things about yourself, but holds back the negatives?

Most women say they would like to meet someone who is a good listener, but on a scale of 1 to 10, how much listening do you want them to do? Do you want a 10, someone who never says anything but listens raptly to every word out of your mouth? Or do you prefer a 5 or 6, who does half the talking and half the listening?

With respect to personal habits, on a scale of 1 to 10, how much drinking would your ideal man do? Likewise for cigarettes, cigars, and pipes. Which drugs, if any, would he enjoy, and how often?

Everyone says they want someone intelligent, but how intelligent would you like him to be? Could you be happy with a genius? Studies reveal that couples that are intellectually incompatible are unlikely to have a happy relationship.

How much money would he have? What would be his net worth or yearly income? Would he be a Trump-like billionaire? Or might you be happier with someone of more modest means?

How old would your ideal partner be? Write down an age range, from youngest you would consider to oldest. Go against the flow and consider someone younger, the younger the better. Remember the earlier section about the advantages of marrying a younger man.

On a more intimate level, everyone says they want someone who enjoys sex. But the important question is are how OFTEN does he want sex? This brings to mind the classic *Annie Hall* movie, where the Woody Allen character complains to his psychiatrist that Annie NEVER wants sex (only once a week) while Annie laments to her shrink that Woody ALWAYS wants sex (once a week). Along with frequency, the other critical question is what varieties of sexual activity does he prefer? One person's fantasy is another person's perversion. So, assuming you can keep your *Wish List* private from curious eyes, be specific about what you want sexually.

Romantic goals are also vital. If you seek marriage and he wants to play the field, this relationship is not going to be satisfying for you. The children question is also vital. How many children (if any) does he want? And crucially, if your biological clock is ticking, HOW SOON does he want kids? Does he already have children, and if so how many? Has he been married before (how many times?) and he is legally single now?

Checklist

Here is a list of other qualities that you may want to include on your *Wish List*. Next to each one, write a number, 1 to 10. There are no right or wrong answers. This is YOUR list. Make sure you include EVERYTHING you need to be in a happy relationship:

- Educated
- Gregarious

- Compassionate
- Emotionally Expressive
- Generous
- Kind
- Monogamous
- Honest
- Funny
- Serious
- Optimistic/Pessimistic
- Listener/Talker
- Self-confident
- Wimp/Macho
- Outgoing/Shy
- Cheap/Spendthrift
- Hard Worker/Fun Loving
- Casual dresser/Formal dresser
- Wants Marriage/Commitment Phobic
- Womanizer/Faithful Type
- Vegetarian/Meat Lover
- Dummy/Genius
- Strong
- Physically Healthy
- Psychologically Healthy
- Independent/Dependent
- Neat/Sloppy
- Morning Person/Night Person
- Party Animal/Homebody
- Mechanically Inclined/Two left thumbs
- Tall/Short (in feet and inches)
- Skinny/Fat
- Muscular
- Athletic
- Hobbies/Fun Activities
- Liberal/Conservative
- Democrat/Republican/Third Party/Independent

- Christian/Jewish/Muslim/Hindu/Agnostic/Atheist
- Church Attendance
- Domestic Travel
- International Travel

Finally, add anything else you consider to be important. Don't leave out interests and hobbies and activities you hope to share with your significant other. Again, be specific. Instead of "Likes Movies," write down "Likes Tearjerker movies (or Romantic Movies or Musicals or Action Movies). Instead of "likes music," write down "lives classical music (or Latin music or hip-hop, or R&B or Top 40 or Techno or House music)."

Here are some other important questions:

1. Where does he live? If he resides far away, are you willing to relocate?
2. What is his religion?
3. What is his racial or ethnic background?
4. What are his parents like? Remember, they are going to be your in-laws.
5. Does he have pets? If so, how many? Does he have to be open to having YOUR pets reside with you if you move in together? Are you willing to give up your cat, if he is allergic?

The Perfect Is the Enemy of the Good

Now comes the hard part. Take that lengthy *Wish List* and boil it down to a short *Must List*, that only includes qualities you MUST have in order to be happy. Go down each of the qualities on your *Wish List* and cross out all the traits you can live without. How long should your *Must List* be? That depends on how long you are willing to wait to meet the love of your life. The longer your *Must List*, the longer the wait. Or the more men you will have to meet before you find someone who has everything you need. As the proverb goes, "The perfect is the enemy of the good." Don't miss out on so many great bachelors out there because of a fruitless search for perfection.

The Compatibility Myth

Get over the fantasy of marrying someone who loves everything you love to do. You don't have to do everything together. Not only is it unrealistic, spending too much time with each other can put as much of a strain on a relationship as too little. Don't expect a man to accompany you to the opera, symphony, or ballet, unless he enjoys them. That's what your BFFs are for! Likewise, don't feel compelled to go to wrestling or boxing matches, or baseball, football, basketball, hockey, or soccer games just to be your man's companion. If you are not into sports, he (and you) will have a much better time if you stay home and permit him to enjoy the "manly sports" with his buddies.

What makes for a lasting, loving, happy relationship? You've heard it over and over, and it's true: COMMUNICATION. If you communicate well with a man you are half way to a successful relationship. Sure, there's still a lot of conflict and struggle in romantic partnerships, but if you listen to one another and communicate clearly and fully and honestly, the odds are in your favor!

One area of compatibility is crucial, however. You have to have compatible COMMUNICATION STYLES. Just about everyone says they want someone who is calm during disagreements and expresses their feelings honestly. But if you have a calm, quiet communication style and he is an angry screamer, your relationship will never work, no matter how many couples therapists you enrich. If he sweeps disagreements under the rug and you want to discuss relationship problems openly, both of you will be unhappy and dissatisfied. Convincing research reveals that of the three basic communication styles, you should choose someone who embraces the same one that you do:

1. Conflict Avoiding
2. Open Discussion of Problems
3. Aggressive or angry discussion of problems

In other words, if you are screamer, marry a screamer. If you don't wind up killing each other, you will get your feelings out and probably make up passionately in the bedroom. Likewise, if you are both good at openly discussing your disagreements in a nonjudgmental way, your relationship is likely to be a happy one. And if neither of you can handle conflict, you may blissfully ignore your problems and pretend that all is perfect.

Don't Make Snap Judgments

It's easy to jump to conclusions about a stranger on the basis of one or more clues. For example, we conclude that someone who is smiling is a happy, friendly, safe man. However, Ted Bundy, the mass murderer, had a lovely smile. A man with a frown on his face may not be unhappy or mean, he just might be having a bad day. We might conclude that a guy with low energy on a first date is boring, whereas he might not be feeling well, or perhaps he has been through the wringer at the office earlier in the day. If an otherwise attractive man has one apparent flaw, you might want to give him the benefit of the doubt and spend a little more time with him.

Being selective is not a shortcoming. But some women exclude entire classes of men for reasons such as race or ethnic origin. If you exclude men out of hand solely because they are African American, Hispanic, Asian, Caucasian, Jewish, or Arab, you are depriving yourself of millions of potential matches. It's true that relationships between different races and ethnic groups can be challenging, especially regarding acceptance by your loved ones and social circles. But a special man is worth it.

Likewise, don't dismiss a man immediately because he doesn't fulfill your fantasy. If he's shorter or taller; darker or lighter than your ideal, give him a chance. Susan Page, author of the best-seller *If I'm So Wonderful, Why Am I Still Single*, loves to tell the story of her initial meeting with her husband-to-be, which was arranged by a well-meaning friend. Susan fantasized about a man with a full head of hair, "like Ted Koppel." Someone well-educated, "preferably with a doctorate." And so forth. When she met her blind date she immediately noticed that he was bald. Strike One. Then she found out that "I only went to community college. Then I dropped out." Strike Two. Fortunately she persisted in the conversation and Strike Three never came.

Men Are Unlikely to Change

A wise proverb states that "Men marry a woman hoping she will stay the same; while women marry a man hoping to change him." Both ends of the proverb lead to unhappy relationships and divorce. If you aren't happy with a man exactly the way he is, warts and all, you are going to be miserable when you discover all the negative qualities he has been hiding from you during the courtship phase. He is going to be on his best behavior as he woos you, but after he settles into marriage, everything he has been suppressing will come out.

Taking Inventory of Yourself

As painful as it is to give up many of the fantasies on your Wish List, now comes the most painful part of this chapter: looking in the mirror and asking, "Do I have what it takes to attract a man with all the qualities on my *Must List*?" Sadly, many of us have unrealistic expectations. Going back to the 1 to 10 scale, most people wind up marrying someone close to themselves in terms of attractiveness. Beautiful people marry beautiful people. The wealthy end up with the wealthy. It is unrealistic for a 3 to expect to marry a 9. If you are unrealistic in your expectations, you may have to go back to your *Must List* and cross off a few more qualities, in order to have a more realistic chance of success. But be careful not to go off the deep end and discard qualities that you find critical. Better to be happily single for the rest of your life than to over-compromise and settle for someone with whom you will spend a lifetime of misery!

Bear in mind that someone who is a 10 in one category might attract someone who is a 10 in another. Melania Trump was penniless when she came to America, but her beauty allowed her to attract a billionaire. Arthur Miller, the homely looking Pulitzer Prize winning playwright, married the greatest sex symbol in world history, Marilyn Monroe. An average looking woman with a great personality might attract a hunk.

The Law of Supply and Demand

In a capitalistic economy such as America's, prices are usually determined by the law of supply and demand. The more scarce a product, the higher the price. Likewise, the greater demand for a product, the higher the price. If you are only attracted to men who are in short supply and high demand, you must be able to pay the price. In this instance, the price you can pay is based on your attractiveness level: physically, intellectually, emotionally, financially, etc. Alas, many women who are less attractive than most still cling to the fantasy of attracting the man who literally is one in a million. The average looking woman may fantasize about marrying the handsome physician, even though he likely has his pick of young, attractive nurses. Even beautiful women may find the competition to be too fierce for wealthy and powerful alpha males like Donald Trump or extremely handsome men.

Here's a strategy for you to consider: why not search for men who are loving, kind, generous, fun, loyal, intelligent, and honest, but who are NOT in great demand? There are millions of good men in America who are unattached because they cannot compete with the men who are in greatest demand. In the first chapter of this book we discussed the qualities personified by President Trump that many women find irresistible. Why not look for the ANTITHESIS of Donald Trump, someone for whom there is very little demand and very great supply?

Younger is Better

One of the biggest mistakes most women make is to marry an older man, even though the average American female lives five years longer than her male counterpart. So unless you want to increase your chances of widowhood, choose a younger man! Furthermore, there is a much greater supply of younger bachelors than older. This is particularly true as women age. This problem is exacerbated by the fact that as men age, they tend to pursue women much younger than themselves. The solution is to give preference to younger men, many of whom would love to date an older woman. Personal Note: I have produced over two thousand singles parties worldwide, with different themes. My Cougar Parties, for younger men/older women, often attract two or three men (cubs) for every cougar! While it is true that most men prefer younger women, there are still millions of younger men who fantasize about attracting their own cougar!

Granted, it's true that on average older men have more money than younger men, but as noted earlier, money is demonstrably NOT the key to happiness. Compare the financial advantage of older men to all the advantages of younger men, who tend to have a higher energy level and also are more likely to view women as their equals. Best of all, cougars will tell you that many older men are set in their ways, whereas younger men are TRAINABLE.

Another advantage to younger men is that they are at the height of their sexual powers at age 16, whereas women do not hit their prime until their forties. Clearly nature intended for women to date their juniors, not their seniors!

Unlike America, where President Trump is 13 years older than wife Melania, France has gone a different direction. Older women dating younger men has been a common French dating phenomenon for quite some time. The current president, Emmanuel Macron, is 25 years older than his lovely wife, Brigitte Trogneau.

After Ivana Trump, our president's first wife, was dumped by The Donald, she came to her senses. Her other ex-husband, Rossano Rubicondi, was 23 years younger. Her current boyfriend (Mark Rota) is ten years younger.

But America is catching up with the French. Ever since Demi Moore married Ashton Kutcher, 16 years her junior, in 2005, the news media has been fascinated by the cougar phenomenon. Today, cougar dating is no longer considered to be unusual. Many female celebrities prefer men often much younger than themselves, particularly Madonna, prefers men "three decades younger" than herself. Other famous cougars include Sharon Stone, Robin Wright, Vivica Fox, Sandra Bullock, Cameron Diaz, Mariah Carey, Nicole Scherzinger, Susan Sarandon, Katie Couric, Sam Taylor-Wood, Jennifer Anniston, Courtney Cox (star of *Cougar Town*), Halle Berry, Paris Hilton, Eva Longoria, Julianne Moore, Jennifer Lopez, Gabrielle Union, Kathy Griffin, Janet Jackson, Eva Mendes, Linda Bollea, Cher, Kim Cattral, Bo Derek, Barbara Hershey, Paula Abdul, Sheryl Crow, Mira Sorvino… The list goes on!

Lest you think cougar dating is only a recent phenomenon, bear in mind that there have been many famous cougars throughout history, including Queen Elizabeth I, Catherine the Great, Khadijah (wife of the prophet Mohammed), Eleanor of Aquitaine, Mae West, and Elizabeth Taylor, just to mention a few.

Do cougar/cub relationships last? Sadly Demi divorced Ashton and many other cougar relationships have foundered. But that's just as true with couples of the same age, according to one study.

While it's common for men like Donald Trump to dump their wives as they age, older women are also divorcing "their ageing hubbies, who have surrendered to beer bellies, man boobs, and boringness," writes Kathy Lette in *The Sydney Morning Herald*, June 11, 2017. "When a girl-friend tells me she wants to get rid of her unsightly fat, there's a good chance she's referring to her couch-potato husband." Ouch!

There are many cougar dating websites. The largest is *CougarLife.com*. My cougar website is CougarEvents.com.

Don't Cut SHORT Your Options

"Tall, dark, and handsome" describes the ideal man for many women. Especially if you are a woman who likes to dress up and wear heels, you may consider a tall man to be ideal. But the demand for tall men is great, while the supply is short. Only 10% of American men, for example, are over six feet, although you would conclude otherwise if you believed online profiles on the web. Short men literally are OVERLOOKED by most women. If you came across a wonderful short man who had everything on your *Must List*, would you veto him purely on the basis of his height? Wouldn't it be easier to just sacrifice the heels, which are terrible for your feet?

Money Isn't Everything

Wealthy men like Donald Trump have their pick of women. Men in high income occupations (doctors, lawyers, executives) likewise are in tremendous demand. Competing for them can be discouraging, if you are not young, slim, and beautiful. Personal Note: I owned a video dating company back in the 80s, when they were considered avant garde. During interviews with prospective female clients I would ask how much money a man had to earn to qualify as a romantic prospect. Most answered, "I don't care." So I would ask, would you date an unemployed man?" "Of course not, " they all answered. Literally, I never met a woman who would consider dating an unemployed man. "Would you marry a man who earned half of your income?" The answer again was always no. Eventually, after some hemming and hawing, they would usually say they wanted to meet a man "who earns at least as much as I do, preferably more."

Perhaps it is unrealistic to expect women to reject thousands of years of conditioning, but let's try anyway. At the risk of sounding like a broken record, Money is NOT the key to happiness. There may be millions of great guys out there who earn less than you do. Versus the exceedingly small number of wealthy men who struggle to find female companionship on a Saturday night. Do the math! A good man becomes EASY to find if you don't require him to earn more money than you, particularly if you have a high income.

Brains and Education Are NOT the Same

It's true that couples that are intellectually incompatible are less likely to be happy and stay together. But what does that have to do with education? Donald Trump "went to the best schools" and certainly is bright, but according to news accounts he seldom reads and gets most of his information by "watching the shows." There is no shortage of bachelors in America who skipped college in order to earn a living, but who are voracious readers and intellectually stimulating. Don't judge a man by his degree, but rather by his intellectual curiosity. Personal Note: A couple of times a year I produce Advanced Degrees Parties for singles with a Doctorate or Masters Degree. The male-female ratio, as you might guess, is always a bad one for women, who tend to be attracted to well-educated men. Consider a less-educated man, and the supply of eligibles goes up, while the competition goes down.

Beta Is Better

The Leader of the Pack, The Alpha Male, by definition is in short supply. He is the one member of the group who leads. There are many followers. So according to the Law of Supply and Demand, you are greatly limiting your choices, and increasing the competition from other women, by pursuing the Alpha Male. On the other hand, Beta Males, the followers, are in plentiful supply, and there is much less competition for them. If a man has to be Captain of the Football Team, Homecoming King, or Captain of Industry to stir your juices, you are in trouble. There's nothing wrong with marrying a good guy who doesn't need to head the parade.

Shy Guys Should Finish First, Not Last

In theory only a small percentage of women prefer a womanizer like President Trump. The vast majority claim they want a man who will be faithful to them. But look at what they do, not what they say. Womanizers, sometimes referred to as Bad Boys, have no shortage of women who fawn on them, only to be discarded when the next pretty face comes along. Many women find the self-confident lady's man to be irresistible. Don't make that mistake. Resist. Choose a man who may be less magnetic, but who has the CHARACTER to be an excellent mate. If you look carefully you will find that there is a much greater supply (and less demand for) true-blue men than there are Don Juans.

Admit it, all of us stare at ourselves in the mirror from time to time. But most of us don't take it to the extreme of Donald Trump and his endless self-promotion. As with womanizers, most women don't believe they want a narcissist for a husband. But sadly, all too often they ignore the shy guys, because they are literally sitting along the outskirts of the room, while the narcissist holds court in the center, with surrounding female hearts a fluttering.

Dr. Philip Zimbardo, Director of The Shyness Institute at Stanford University, is the world's foremost authority on shyness. He claims that 40% of people are basically shy. Now most of us are shy at least some of the time, but the 40% Dr. Zimbardo refers to are people who are generally always shy in social situations with strangers. These men often make great husbands, because they are just as much into you as they are into themselves. They tend to be good listeners. And they are unlikely to cheat on you. The only negative (to some) is that they are shy. If you truly can't bear to be around a shy guy, then obviously this an option that is not open to you. But if you can get over society's prejudice against shy men, you will find a tremendously overlooked resource in the dating market. You don't have to young, slim, and beautiful to attract a shy man. You just have to do what most women fail to do: notice him and take the initiative to meet him. More on that later...

One myth that is often repeated is that many beautiful women are home alone on Saturday night because nobody asked them out. The truth is that beautiful women get asked out all the time. The problem is that the wrong men approach them. The Donald Trumps of the world are never too shy to try to pick up a gorgeous lady. But the best men are often the shyest. And you will never meet them if you wait for them to make the first move.

A Good Man Is EASY to Find

As long as you pursue men who are in short supply but in great demand, you will find that "a good man is hard to find." But if you are willing to broaden your horizons and at least consider the millions of shorter, poorer, less-educated, shy, beta males, you will find there is no shortage of great guys available who are overlooked in favor of the Donald Trumps of the world.

PART 4

The Right Bait

Wouldn't it be great if men judged you, as Dr. Martin Luther King, Jr. would say, "by the content of your character," rather than your looks? As wonderful as that would be, it's not a realistic expectation.

Men are superficial when choosing a romantic partner. You are unlikely to win a man unless he finds you to be physically attractive. So it is imperative to do everything in your power to improve your appearance.

When a man first sees you, he can only see what he can see. So he will judge you initially 100% on the basis of your appearance. Intelligence, kindness, loving nature, and humor are all invisible qualities. So what are most bachelors looking for? Personal Note: Writing a successful dating book can be challenging for a male author, because most customers of this genre are female. If a male dating expert is totally honest about describing his own sex, it's easy to dismiss him as a male chauvinist. I noticed that female dating experts and authors at my singles events could discuss the most depressing aspects of male superficiality, without provoking anger from women in the audience. But if I said the same thing, I was in deep trouble. How's that for a double standard?

Once a man gets to know you, your inner beauty is essential for him to choose you for a significant relationship. But you have to get to first base. That's where the image you present is paramount.

Below are some suggestions on how to package yourself to make a good first impression on a man. Some women object to having to change their appearance. A man can take or leave her. Unfortunately, often he will do just that: leave you.

Appearing to be Younger

Donald Trump is not the only man who prefers younger women. Of course he takes this to an extreme, but most men are attracted to younger women. Even beautiful actresses in Hollywood find that their movie roles dry up when they hit 40. The younger you look, the greater the odds that the average guy will be attracted to you. When a man first sees you, he doesn't know your age. But he will guess. It is in your best interest that he guess low. It's better to be a 40 year old woman who looks 30, than a 30 year old who looks 40, at the initial encounter. He won't know your true age, unless you foolishly volunteer it. When should you give him the "bad news" that you are older than he thought? After you hear the magic words, "I love you." Once you have captured his heart, age truly becomes just a number. But if he had known ahead of time your true age, he might not have given you the chance to reveal the wonderful person you are. Personal Note: Any man who asks your age is being rude. At my singles events it happens. Or even worse, men may even ask your weight. Crazy. By the way, it is just as rude to ask a man how much money he makes, which I am told is asked frequently at my parties. Generally, most people of both sexes are superficial, but they are superficial about different things. Many men fantasize about young women who are way beyond their league. Many women dream about the Trump-like billionaire. Neither sex has a monopoly on superficiality.

Grey Hair

This a real sore point with many women. "All my friends tell me I look great with grey hair!" Yes, but how many of them are MEN? Everyone knows the double standard: Men with grey hair are considered to be "distinguished;" women who are grey are just plain "old." To maximize the number of men you will attract, consider dyeing your hair. If it's just too much trouble, or you find this double standard to be offensive (which woman doesn't!) then keep your grey locks. Just don't be surprised if your options are limited because of this.

Makeup

We all laugh at the teeny bopper and her first experiments with cosmetics. Women can certainly look silly if they apply too much makeup. But too little can also be a problem. Most men swear they hate makeup, but as the adage goes, "Look at what they do, not what they say." Men tend to be attracted to women with smooth skin, luscious lips, and beautiful eyes and lashes. You are blessed if you naturally have these characteristics. But if you are like the vast majority of women, cosmetics, tastefully applied, can greater increase your attractiveness to the opposite sex. If you are not gifted in this area, ask a friend to teach you. Or better yet, go to a free seminar at the cosmetics section of your favorite department store.

Weight Loss

We live in a society obsessed with slimness almost to the point of anorexia. The feminine ideal is the supermodel, whose figure is totally unrealistic for everyone other than the tiniest percentage. The first step for most people (male and female) is to lose weight.

So how do you lose weight? First and foremost, if you are on a diet, get off it! Some studies reveal that less than 4% of the population can both lose a significant amount of weight and keep it off through dieting. For most people dieting only leads to the yo-yo effect of gaining and losing hundreds of pounds over a lifetime. What's the alternative? Don't go on a diet, but instead CHANGE your diet. Starving yourself for a month can lead to fast weight loss, but it is ineffective long-term. If you change your diet permanently to healthier foods, you will both live longer and lose weight and, more importantly, keep it off.

Why do so many of us have trouble controlling our weight? One major cause is the easy availability of delicious, affordable, convenient food in most of the developed world. All you can eat buffets are prevalent and ridiculously affordable. It's no wonder that we face a crisis of obesity. Developed nations, again especially the United States, share another serious problem: the lack of time.

Is there a connection between these twin phenomena of Obesity and Lack of Time? Is it just a coincidence that the United States leads the world in both areas: one of the most obese and the most workaholic nations on the earth? Lack of time, due to poor time management, leads almost inevitably to obesity. The good news is that careful Time Management can lead to less stress, more enjoyment of life, and a slimmer waistline. Here's how:

Sleep

Most Americans are chronically sleep-deprived. According to the National Sleep Foundation, the average adult needs between seven and nine hours of sleep per night. However, the *Sleepless in America Poll of 2005* revealed that the average American only gets 6.85 hours of sleep each night. This leads to weight gain, because the longer you are awake, the greater the temptation to eat. This is particularly true late at night, when people get the "munchies." After working or playing until the wee hours of the morning (for example, nightclubbing), most people get hungry. So they have that extra snack or go out for an early breakfast. Those extra calories could easily have been avoided by going to bed earlier.

The fact is that every waking hour is an opportunity for eating and gaining weight. Conversely, you consume zero calories while you are asleep. Therefore, the more hours you sleep, the less you eat, and the less weight you gain.

Why do most people sleep less than they should? One major reason is that people don't place enough emphasis on the value of sleep. They think that working a long day or partying until all hours of the night are higher priorities than sleeping. And they pay the price with a bulging waistline.

So the first step in losing weight is to schedule seven to nine hours of uninterrupted sleep each night.

Exercise

Just about everyone realizes the advantages of exercise. So why do we exercise so little? One common excuse is "that I don't have time." Exercising can be time-consuming, especially if you follow the recommendations of experts, who prescribe vigorous aerobic exercise at least 3-4 times a week. If you like to exercise in the gym, add the time required to leave your home to get there, plus showering, hair styling, and applying makeup after your workouts. So it's understandable that most people don't exercise regularly, as revealed by their flabby physiques.

Most experts insist that a successful weight control program must include regular exercise. Putting all of your eggs in one basket, changing your diet, is a recipe for failure.

What is the best exercise for you? Any exercise that you enjoy. If exercise is a chore, you will gradually lose motivation, and stop altogether. Pick at least one fun activity, and perform it regularly.

1. Competitive sports, such as tennis, basketball, golf (without the cart, of course), basketball, volleyball, racquetball, etc, are great. Your local recreation department sponsors numerous fun sports, from volleyball to softball.
2. Water sports. Swimming, kayaking, canoeing, surfing.
3. Joining a health club, gym, or YMCA is also a great way to expend calories with new friends.
4. Walking or hiking are among the best forms of exercise. Even a few minutes a day are good, but if you are serious about losing weight, experts recommend at least 45 minutes per day. A Duke University Study found that 30 minutes a day of walking helped mainly sedentary people maintain their weight, but that they had to walk at least 45 minutes a day to lose weight. Buy a pedometer, which keeps track of the number of steps you take each day. Typically average people only take two or three thousand steps a day. Try to add one or two thousand extra steps and you will lose weight. While walking AFTER dinner is a great habit, walking BEFORE dinner is even better! A university of Glasgow study revealed that 20 minutes of walking reduced appetite.
5. Jogging or running are great exercise, particularly if you are short on time. Speed walking is another way to benefit from exercise when you are on a tight schedule.
6. If you are unwilling to budget four or more hours a week for regular exercise, try doing 100 jumping jacks five times a day. Each set just

takes two minutes, so that's only 10 minutes a day. You'll expend 100 calories each day, adding up to 700 calories each week.

7. Another exercise tip is taking the stairs instead of an elevator. According to The Centers for Disease Control, if you spent ten minutes a day walking up and down stairs, you would lose ten pounds a year (if you kept your calorie intake the same).

8. Parking your car a block or two from work is also helpful. Walking that extra block or two twice a day doesn't expend that much time, but it pays off in weight loss.

9. Housework can also expend lots of calories. 30 minutes of scrubbing expends 120 calories.

The first six steps above have the added benefit of getting you out of the house and hopefully interacting with lots of strangers, close to half of whom are likely to be men!

Diet

All experts recommend a healthy, nutritious, moderate-calorie diet. Unfortunately such a diet takes time and can be quite expensive. Unhealthy high calorie food is much more convenient, and much less costly. Given a choice between cooking a healthy meal at home or eating fast food on the run, most of us visit the golden arches of McDonald's. And the pounds pile on.

Here are some great suggestions for changing your diet.

1. **Eat at home**. Restaurants tend to serve extra-large portions, and tend to include high-fat, high calorie foods. And restaurant menus offer you limited choices. If you cook at home, you have complete control of what and how much you eat. That takes a lot more time: shopping for food, preparing your meals, cleaning up the table and washing dishes. But it is very effective for weight loss. Also, shopping, cooking, and cleaning burn up calories! Plus you'll save a lot of money eating at home.

2. **Eat Breakfast each morning**. Many experts agree that one major key to weight control is eating breakfast. Unfortunately, many of us skip the most important meal of the day. Why? Because our frantic schedules leave no room for a full nutritious breakfast. So we either eat an unhealthy convenient fast-food style breakfast, or we skip breakfast altogether. Again our waistlines expand. Ideally, you will eat more calories BEFORE noon than AFTER noon. Studies reveal that if you eat more before noon, you will eat less in the evening. What's the best breakfast for you? A high-protein breakfast of eggs is one possibility. Mixing in sautéed spinach, chopped tomatoes, and shredded reduced-fat cheese are great additions to your eggs. Other great breakfast choices are high-fiber, low sugar, whole-grain cereals such as oatmeal or bran; or nonfat yogurt topped with berries, chopped apples or chopped walnuts. If you must eat breakfast at a fast-food restaurant, make healthy choices. McDonald's offers Fruit & Maple Oatmeal with low-fat milk, with only 360 calories. Dunkin' Donuts offers an Egg White Turkey Sausage Wrap. Starbucks offers Cherry Yogurt Parfait.

3. **Eat more slowly**. Lack of time causes us to eat too fast, which leads to overeating. Experts contend that it takes time (at least twenty minutes) for the body to register that it has eaten enough calories. If we eat too fast, we end up consuming more calories than we should. The solution is to slow down and chew our food thoroughly. This gives our brains time to catch up with our caloric consumption and realize that we have eaten enough. One way to eat more slowly is to put your fork down between bites. Also, sip water frequently and converse with your dining partners throughout your meals.

4. **Eat more often**. Experts recommend five small meals or snacks per day, rather than two or three large meals. This involves a lot more time, but it's worth it.

5. **Invest time to form new friendships** with people with good eating and exercise habits and then spend as much time as possible with them. Spend less time with sedentary friends and family. Their bad habits will become yours.

6. **Find a Weight-Loss buddy**. They can be face-to-face or online. Encourage each other to stick to your weight loss program.

7. **Keep a Journal** that lists everything you eat each day and approximate calorie counts. TV's favorite health guru, Dr. Oz, cites studies that reveal that you will lose twice as much weight if your keep track of your calories. You'll be surprised by how many more calories you consume that you thought! The Journal will keep you conscious of your food choices and help you choose more wisely.

8. **Spend your time being busy**, rather than laying around the house all day. Bored people eat more. If family and career don't fill your days, develop new hobbies and pastimes. Remember, the more time you spend out of the house, the more men you are likely to meet!

9. **Take the time to read food labels**. The first ingredients listed are the ones that predominate. Avoid foods that list sugar, fructose, or corn syrup as the first few ingredients. Substitute sugar-free varieties of your favorite foods, including ketchup, mayonnaise, and salad dressing.

10. **Watch less television**. The more you watch the more you eat. Go for a walk instead!

Creating the Time to Lose Weight

We all begin with an equal amount of time: 24 hours per day. Some of us choose to spend that time with healthy activities and choices that lead to weight control. Others choose activities that lead to weight gain. But the difference is not that we have unequal amounts of time, but rather, different priorities. If you are having difficulty controlling your weight, it is likely that you have other priorities more important to you: earning more money, educating yourself, having fun. These are all worthwhile pursuits, but you won't lose significant amounts of weight unless that also becomes a major priority.

As discussed earlier, the almighty dollar is the main motivator in America, and people will go to great lengths to earn it. Their actions clearly indicate that they believe that money is paramount in the pursuit of happiness. Other goals are much lower on the priority ladder, particularly weight control, which as we have seen, requires a tremendous investment in time. So rather than forego earning money, we sacrifice our health and trim waistlines.

Studies of happiness reveal that there is indeed a correlation between money and happiness. But it's a SMALL correlation. The fact is that there are millions of happy poor people and millions more who are prosperous and miserable. Ask yourself this question: would my life be better if I had more money or a healthier, slimmer body? In an ideal world we could choose both. Unfortunately, most people find that the more time they invest in making money, the less they have for weight control; and vice versa. So unless you are one of the lucky people who are financially secure and need not work another day, you have to choose. Hopefully you will make the healthy choice. Not only will your life be happier, it will likely be longer.

Changing Your Diet

It's a truism that "diets don't work." Studies reveal that up to 96% of people who go on a diet either don't lose much weight, or regain it quickly. The main reason for this may be that your body interprets a diet as starvation. If you deprive yourself of sufficient calories, your body panics and concludes that is starving to death. So your body drops its metabolic rate and spends calories at a slower, miserly rate. Your body will do everything it can to sabotage your diet, because of its desire to continue living. The secret is to CHANGE your diet, rather than go on a diet based on deprivation. Here are some suggestions:

1. **Drink lots of water**. Water is free, healthy, and has ZERO calories. Water fills your stomach, giving you a sense of being full, so you are less likely to eat. It is a terrific alternative to sodas and fruit juices, which contain high calories. The average American gets 245 calories a day from soft drinks, which adds up to 25 pounds a year! Drinking ice water is particularly valuable, because your body expends calories heating the water!

2. **Each more spicy foods**. Substitute pepper for salt. Add hot sauce, salsa, etc. to your food. Spices cause your body to burn more calories. Hot peppers reduce your appetite.

3. **Eat on smaller plates and drink out of smaller glasses**. We have a tendency to eat everything on our plate and drink everything in our glass, so the smaller plates and glasses will result in less calories.

4. **Sit in front of a mirror when you eat**. One study revealed that people ate one-third less, just from this one tip.

5. **Eat more fruits and vegetables**. This is not only healthier, it leads to considerable weight loss. Fruits and vegetables fill up your stomach, so there's less room for higher-calories foods. Fruits and vegetables contain high fiber and water content, effective weapons in the war on flab! Soups and salads also have high water content.

6. **Substitute whole fruit for fruit juices**. For the same amount of calories, you eat something that is much more filling.

7. **Avoid white**. White bread, white rice, white sugar all can be replaced by whole grain breads and brown rice.

8. **Drink non-fat milk**. If you are used to drinking whole milk, it takes a while to adjust to non-fat. Eventually you won't miss the fatty milk.

9. **Eat low-fat yogurt**.

10. **Eliminate alcohol from your diet**. Alcoholic drinks are high calorie. If you are unwilling to give up beer, drink a lite beer if you want to avoid the dreaded "beer belly." Wine usually has fewer calories than mixed drinks. In restaurants and lounges order by glass rather than by the bottle. You'll drink less.

11. **Eat only when your stomach is growling**. Just because you crave some calories doesn't mean your body is actually hungry. You could be eating out of nervousness or boredom. If you are desperate to eat a specific type of food, it probably means you aren't really hungry and don't need those calories! On the other hand, if you are willing to eat just about anything, that's a sure sign that you are really hungry.

12. **Substitute low-calorie snacks**, such as almonds, for those that are sugary.

13. **Eat frozen dinners** that are designed specifically for those seeking to lower their weight.
14. **Avoid late night snacks**. This can save you 300 calories or more a day, or 31 pounds a year.
15. **Order salad dressing on the side**. Stick your fork into the salad dressing first, then into the salad. The dressing often contains more calories than the salad itself!
16. **Carry low-fat snacks** with you throughout the day, such as trail mix or small carrots. You'll be less tempted to turn to less healthy choices.
17. **Order smaller portions** at the restaurant, stadium, or theatre. Whether it's a sub sandwich, fries, or popcorn, you usually have a choice in sizes. Since we tend to each whatever is in front of us, smaller portions lead to less calories.
18. **Buy yourself a new wardrobe** when you lose weight. And throw away your old, baggy clothes. You will be more reluctant to regain the weight if it means having to buy still another wardrobe!

Appearances Can Be Everything

What do you do if you are unable or unwilling to lose weight? The good news is that you don't actually have to lose weight. A substitute is to APPEAR thinner.

Wardrobe

Start with your wardrobe. Choose colors and fashions that slim you down. It's common knowledge that dark colors make you look thinner. That's why the majority of women at social events wear black. Other than on your wedding day, avoid white, unless you are one of the lucky ones who looks good in white. Wear clothes with vertical rather than horizontal stripes. And wearing heels is the easiest way to appear to be ten pounds thinner.

Of course heels are bad for your feet. And disguising excess weight is a poor substitute for actually losing weight, which will not only make you more attractive, but also more healthy. So take another look at the advice above for losing weight. The greatest reward for losing weight is not that you will attract Mr. Right, but that you will but will live a healthier, happier, longer life.

Contact Lenses

Some men like eyeglasses on a woman. But they are the minority. Contact lenses will maximize the number of bachelors from whom to choose.

Perfume

Don't. It's as simple as that. Many men (and women) are allergic to perfume. They will scratch you off their lists immediately, unless you are beautiful.

Smoking

Matchmakers used to report that matching their overweight clients was the greatest challenge. No more. Smokers are now the most difficult to match. In some parts of the U.S., smoking is declining to less than 15% of the population. You lose a lot of prospects in the dating pool if you smoke. Even smokers, especially those who are hoping to quit, often prefer non-smokers, the rationale being "I'll never be able to give up smoking if I marry a smoker."

Smoking also ages the skin. Plus, smoke smells bad to non-smokers. So give it up, if at all possible. There are numerous stop smoking drugs, devices, seminars, and organizations for you to consider. If capturing a great guy isn't sufficient motivation, consider the prospect of being afflicted with cancer. Cigarettes are bad news, from almost any perspective.

Rings

Many women love rings. Some wear several. Big mistake. Most men are not the most observant. They see a ring or rings on your fingers and conclude you are taken. "But don't they know the difference between an engagement/wedding ring from just a nice piece of jewelry?" No, many don't.

Teeth

Now, more than ever, it's essential to have attractive teeth. Missing teeth can be a deal-breaker, right off the bat. Yellowed teeth, due to aging or smoking, are also damaging to your prospects. Consider investing time, money, and maybe some physical pain into getting your teeth capped, whitened, replaced, or straightened. Personal Note: I knew a woman who was reluctant to smile because she had crooked teeth. She developed a complex. It greatly inhibited her dating life. In her late 20s she visited the orthodontist. She looked silly in braces for a while. But it revolutionized her self-image and enabled her to break out of her shell and begin dating with confidence. Eventually it led to marriage.

Personal Hygiene

Some obvious things have to be discussed, just to ensure they don't get overlooked. Daily bathing, clean clothes, and dental hygiene are essential to successful dating.

Truth in Packaging

Don't listen to men who condemn makeup and pushup bras as being dishonest. It is likely that they also use tricks like combovers, lifts in their shoes, wearing boots, etc.

The #1 Secret to Looking Great

Enhancing your appearance can require a lot of work, money, and pain (plastic surgery, for example.) You may not have the self-discipline to exercise regularly and change your diet. But there is one thing everyone can do that requires little effort and no money. You can smile. A tiny percentage of the population looks beautiful without a smile. They earn big bucks as fashion models and movie stars. The rest of us mere mortals need a little help. Smiling literally DOUBLES your attractiveness. Any photographer will tell you that the secret to making your customer look good is to get her/him to smile. That's why the number one word in a photographer's vocabulary is "cheese."

PART 5
How to Meet Good Men

Men's Dirty Little Secret

Most men love to play the macho game. They go to great lengths to appear strong, masculine, courageous. But deep inside they hide a secret. They are scared to death of being rejected. They would rather risk being alone for a lifetime than take a chance of being turned down by an attractive woman.

Here's a fun exercise. Some Saturday night when there's nothing on TV you want to view, go to your local hot spot and watch the men. They are pathetic. The average man in a singles bar meets zero women in an evening. You can see them chatting with their buddies at the bar while they secretly are scoping the room for women they find attractive who appear to be single. After a sufficient amount of liquid courage, they cross the room and ask a woman to dance. And then disaster strikes. The woman says no. Now the poor fellow must slink back to his buddies, terrified that everyone in the bar has witnessed his moment of humiliation. The average guy who gets rejected just this one time usually decides to leave ("All the women in this bar are stuck up!) Or if he is the courageous type, he returns to the bar and orders a double. So much for male courage.

If there is one thing all single women need to understand, it is how overpowering this fear of rejection is for most men. And if you can't understand this, picture yourself in this scenario. How would you feel if you got rejected in front of dozens of witnesses?

The great tragedy is that the fear of rejection paralyzes most men continuously, every day. And women are the victims, because there are men who are secretly attracted to you, but you will never know, because most will not approach you.

Bearing this in mind, one solution is to signal to an attractive man that he won't be rejected if he approaches you. The most obvious way is to make eye contact with him, just for a second or two. Even better, give him a big smile, before you turn away from him shyly. Best of all, walk over and initiate contact. I know, that really takes guts. But I guarantee you will not have any trouble meeting good men if you are willing to take the initiative.

Lack of accessibility is another cause of men not approaching you. For example, most women sit at a table, if it is available. The table is a barrier to men approaching you. Best to stand, so he can easily start speaking with you.

Perhaps the biggest mistake women make in creating barriers is to travel with bodyguards (your friends) to parties and bars. No man wants to approach two or more women. First of all, he doesn't want to chance being rejected in front of witnesses (who might snicker cruelly). Secondly, most men are too polite to interrupt a conversation. If you are chatting with a girlfriend, a man likely will wait for a lull in the conversation, which unfortunately seldom comes. In most cases, he will have to butt in, which only a very self-confident aggressive man would do (e.g. a man like Trump).

In real estate they say the three most important things are location, location, and location. Doubly true with the singles scene. Locate yourself where every man will see you and can easily speak with you. Sitting or standing at the bar is best. Hiding out in a dark corner, behind a column and/or table, guarantees you will meet very few men, if any.

One more turnoff to men is bad body language, such as crossing your arms or legs. Looking away and refusing to make eye contact is another. Turning your back guarantees you won't meet anyone. These are obvious mistakes that a surprising number of women make, who then complain that no one approached them!

Don't Listen to Mom... and Other Well-Meaning Advisers

Your mom means well. And so do your BFFs. But their advice can often lead to disaster. Just as you shouldn't go to an amateur for medical advice, the same is true for dating advice. The most common example of bad advice is

Never Make the First Move. "If a man is attracted to you, he's going to make the first move. If he doesn't, it means he's not interested." FALSE. 40% of bachelors are painfully shy and are extremely reluctant to approach you. In fact, the MORE attracted they are to you, the LESS likely they are to make the first move. They are more likely to approach a woman they find less attractive than you, thinking there is a lesser chance of rejection. In reality, the opposite is true. One study found that the rejection rate was identical, regardless of the attractiveness level of the women. But most men don't know this. So yes, maybe he isn't approaching you because he finds you unattractive. Or just as likely, he's just plain chicken.

The beauty of approaching shy men is they can choose you... or nobody. If they are shy, they seldom meet women they find attractive. So basically you have a monopoly. There is no competition for shy men. While most of the other single women waste their time trying to flirt with the Donald Trumps of the world, you have the shy men all to yourself, if you are willing to make the first move.

Stalking the Shy Man

When you are at social events, what kind of body language do you display? Are your arms and legs crossed? Is your posture slumped? Are you looking down? These behaviors signal that you are afraid, defensive, unfriendly, or depressed. Most men, especially shy men, will avoid you, no matter how attracted to you they may be. So straighten up, loosen up, and open yourself!

No matter how oblivious to women he may appear to be, shy men want to meet you. They just don't have the guts to make the first move. That means it's up to you. And it's as easy as 1-2-3.

1. **Eye contact**. This is just a euphemism for staring at someone, ideally for at least two seconds. Then avert your eyes demurely. If you stare for less than two seconds, he will convince himself that you don't find him attractive. More than two seconds, he might conclude you are a stalker!

2. **Smile**. So many women walk around with a perpetual frown and wonder why they never meet any men. Any time you are in a social

situation, you should have a smile painted on your face. Women object to this, saying it would be a phony smile. Exactly. You may have to force yourself to smile, but whatever it takes, do it. As the proverb goes, "you catch a lot more flies with honey than with vinegar."

3. **Say something**. Ideally steps 1 and 2 would be enough to get the reluctant bachelor to walk up to you and start a conversation. Unfortunately, no matter how much you stare and smile at men, a high percentage will never start up a conversation with you even if they are 99% convinced you find them attractive. That's how afraid of rejection many of them are. So in these cases, you need to take the initiative and start the conversation.

Opening Lines

Every conversation has to start somewhere. That's called an opening line. Single men pay good money to professional pickup artists to learn the best pickup lines. Some can be quite cheesy. But there are lots of perfectly respectable ways to begin that first conversation.

1. **Ask a question**. "What do you think of the music?" or "Is that A margarita you're drinking?"
2. **Complain**. "They could turn up the air-conditioning in this place!"
3. **Compliment**. "I like Your tie!"
4. **Express a Preference**. "I love this song."

Personal Note: Susan Scott often was the featured speaker at my singles events. One night at a social gathering she used one of the most original opening lines I have ever heard. "Can I buy you a drink or would you prefer the cash?" It turned out to be a very expensive opener. She quickly ran out of money and wound up being unable to pay to retrieve her car from the parking garage). But every man in the room wanted to meet the outrageous woman who was offering free drinks!

What's the best opening line? *Los Angeles* magazine asked that question on the streets of L.A. Do you dare to use it in your town? The number one opener in the city of Los Angeles was "Hi!" You don't have to clever, you don't have to be original, you don't have to be funny. Just say "Hi!"

Personal Note: My favorite opening line when I was single was "Hi, I'm Rich!" The women always went for that one. But that's not how I met my wife. One of my jobs at my singles dances is to fill the dance floor. No one wants to be half of the first couple on the dance floor in a large hotel ballroom or nightclub. So I would start the party by asking different women to dance. Others got the hint, and not long thereafter the party was jumping. Once that happened, it was time for me to look around the room for someone for myself. I had noticed Debby earlier, but hadn't asked her to dance, because she didn't need me to get her onto the dance floor. She took care of that herself. I waited for the right moment, when she wasn't dancing or talking to anyone, and walked across the room. I didn't want to risk rejection, so instead of asking her to dance, I grabbed her hand and pulled her onto the dance floor. I call this "The Caveman Technique." She could dance with me, or suffer a dislocated shoulder. A little over a year later, we were married!

Using Props

Sometimes it's not what you say, but who is with you, that's important. Your dog can be a valuable prop in meeting men. Make sure you take your dog, as often as possible, to a place where there are lots of men passing by. Especially if you have an unusual or beautiful dog, men will stop to ask the breed or name of the dog. Even better, if the guy also has a dog with him, the dogs will introduce themselves to each other, greatly facilitating the owners doing likewise. An added advantage, if you have a large dog, is you will feel safer meeting strangers.

A baby is another great prop. If you don't have one of your own, borrow one from your sister or your neighbor. They will love the free time you are giving them. Everyone loves babies, and men will stop you on the street and ask how old your baby is or compliment her/him. Your reply: "Oh, this isn't my baby, it's my neighbor's."

Conquering Your Own Fear of Rejection

Approaching an attractive man takes guts. That's why so few women do it. Which means you have a tremendous advantage if you are the one who is fearless in approaching men. How do you conquer the fear of rejection? Simple. Go out and get rejected! Personal Note: People who meet me notice immediately that I am an extrovert. But it wasn't always so. Especially with attractive women. I once was the biggest coward in San Francisco—when it came to approaching women. My first date was as a sophomore in college. I was walking out of the classroom one day and bumped into a coed in the hallway. We spoke for a minute, then she moved on to the next classroom. We flirted for a couple of minutes every Monday, Wednesday, and Friday thereafter. I knew she liked me, and I did likewise, but neither us was willing to risk rejection. After a couple of weeks it dawned on me that she never was going to ask me out on a date! I had to initiate, or miss out on my big chance to enter the dating world. Somehow I found the courage to ask her out, and miraculously she said yes. Lucky, otherwise I probably would have run off to join the monastery! (I was a student at the University of San Francisco, a Catholic university).

It would be great if there was a prescription for courage available at the drug store. Alas, repeatedly getting rejected is the only way to conquer that fear. Psychologists have a fancy term for this: desensitization. So make a commitment to yourself to accumulate at least one rejection every time you go to a social event.

Personal Note: Most women at my parties love to dance. They complain bitterly when no one asks them onto the dance floor. "How many men have YOU asked to dance tonight?" I ask. "None" almost always is the answer. My wife Debby attended many singles dances before she met me at one of mine. She had a rule, that she never let a good song go to waste. If she heard one of her favorites and no one approached her fast enough, she asked the closest guy to dance.

Minimizing the Risk

Timing is one key to avoiding rejection. Don't ask a man to dance, for example, if he is putting on his coat and getting ready to leave. Or if he has just ordered a drink and has to wait to pay for it.

Eye contact is another technique that reduces the chances of rejection. Try to make eye contact with a man before approaching him. If he looks away, it may be because he is not attracted to you or is not available. Of course it could also mean that he is painfully shy. If you are a risk-taker, you might go ahead and approach him anyway, in spite of long odds against you.

The Art of Conversation

Regardless of who makes the first move, the next step is keeping the conversation going. This can be difficult, especially if you are with a shy man, or you are the shy type yourself. The worst of both worlds is where both of you are shy. Good luck!

The most important part of that first conversation is remembering the man's first name. Sounds simple, but social anxiety makes it easy to immediately forget his name upon hearing it. Try having a good conversation with a stranger if you forget his first name. Very difficult. A man's name is usually the most beautiful sound in the English language to him. Use it repeatedly in that first conversation, and you create rapport and a sense of intimacy. Forget the name and you are in trouble. One way to remember is repeat the name immediately upon hearing it. "Nice to meet you, Charlie." And then repeat it soon thereafter, so it is imprinted on your brain. One problem you may encounter is that we tend to remember the last thing we hear, and forget what came previously. "Nice to meet you, Charlie; my name is Angie." Guess what, you are likely to remember your name is Angie and forget Charlie's name. Better to say, My name is Angie, what's yours?" followed by "Nice to meet you, Charlie."

Keeping the Conversation Moving

Many men who are shy initially turn out to be motor mouths. The legendary Johnny Carson conversed with thousands of guests on *The Tonight Show*. Regardless of how boring many of them were in their private lives, for fifteen minutes on national TV they were the most scintillating conversationalists in the world. How did he draw them out? He asked them to discuss their favorite topic, the one subject on which they were the foremost authorities: THEMSELVES. It's easy to get a shy man talking. Ask him about himself.

Finding Something in Common

We all feel more comfortable with someone like ourselves. Although we may feel very different from an attractive stranger we have just met, it's amazing how many things we may have in common:

- Play the same card games
- Watch or play the same sports
- Similar hobbies
- Belong to the same church or club
- Know similar people
- Similar family background
- Similar educational background
- Traveled to similar destinations
- Attended the same college
- Read the same authors
- Enjoy the same movies or music
- Appreciate the same artists
- Born in the same town
- Have children of similar ages
- Have similar ambitions or goals
- Admire the same historical figures or modern day heroes

You won't know what you have in common unless you invest time with each other.

How to Be More Interesting

If you are a homebody who doesn't read much, doesn't pay attention to the news, or limits your interactions to your immediate family, you may not be much fun on a date. Nobody wants to spend their lives with a bore. Time to expand your horizons and become a more interesting person. Here's how:

- Get out of the house more
- Spend more time with strangers or people outside your immediate social circle
- Read a daily newspaper. Also weeklies and monthly magazines
- Join a Book Club and/or read the latest best-sellers
- Go out to the latest movies, art exhibits, and exhibitions at museums
- Join clubs

We all have had interesting experiences and we all have heard hilarious jokes. If you are not the best story or joke teller, rehearse. Learn to hold up your end of a conversation, whether you are on a date or in a larger group.

What do you do if your conversation partner has his eyes glazed over? Shake up the conversation by abruptly changing the subject, asking a question, or raising your voice. Or ask, "Am I boring you?" Maybe he didn't get much sleep last night or is distracted by a personal problem. Don't just persist as if there is nothing wrong.

Superficial is Good...at First

You can't expect a meaningful, intimate conversation at the first encounter. People are nervous and often defensive initially, so relax and give him (and yourself) permission to be superficial. No need to begin unveiling all of your problems or ask him for his. And avoid controversial subjects, especially the big three: religion, politics, and sex. Save those discussions for later. There's nothing wrong with discussing the weather or sports, no matter how trite both topics may be. You have start somewhere. Better that it be something safe.

Active Listening

The best conversationalists, for example talk show hosts, aren't necessarily the best talkers. They are the best listeners. Try to let the man do most of the talking in the first conversation. That plays to a man's ego. He naturally is drawn to women who take a real interest in him. It's a compliment to him if you listen with rapt attention and follow up with questions that reveal your interest in him. And why shouldn't you be interested? He may not know it, but he is auditioning for the role of Mr. Right in your life. The more he talks, the more valuable information you glean about him. Silently you are going down your checklist of qualities you seek in a romantic partner, while he enjoys talking about his favorite subject.

The ideal conversation is when both parties have the opportunity to share. Talking too much is just as bad as talking too little. If you have a tendency to monopolize encounters, it is important to take a deep breath and listen. PERSONAL NOTE: As a public speaker since age 9, I like to talk. That was very evident early in my dating career. I found that women often were fascinated with me—for the first half hour. Then my verbal skills became a liability. Being a good listener is far more important than being a good talker. It took me many years (and many overly brief dating relationships) to learn that lesson.

Are you a bad listener? One obvious cause may be poor hearing. As we get older our hearing declines. If you find that you can't hear very well, you may develop the habit of monopolizing the conversation because it's so much work to strain to hear others. The solution is obvious: get a hearing aid.

Do any of these poor listening types describe you?

- Egocentric. Everything has to be about you.
- Constantly interrupting.
- Poor attention span. Instead of listening to others, you plan your day or brood about your problems.
- Motor Mouth. Susan Rabin, author of the best-seller *How to Meet Anyone, Any Time, Any Place,* tells the story of one man who she met through a personal ad who wouldn't let her get a word in edgewise. At the end of the first (and last) date, he complimented her for being such a great conversationalist!

If you are a poor listener, it will greatly reduce your relationship options. Most people want a reasonably equal amount of time to talk, and also need to feel listened to. Make an effort to shut up and really listen, reduce interruptions, focus your attention totally on what he is saying, and ask questions about him.

What do you do with an extremely quiet man? Long silences can be very uncomfortable. You will be tempted to fill in the blanks yourself. Better to realize that every man has an interesting story to tell, and your job is to draw him out by asking questions and, most importantly, listening to the answers. You may also choose to mirror back the conversation ("I hear you saying that...")

Taboo Subjects at First Encounter

Never reveal your troubles and worries and problems in your first conversation with a promising prospect. Unless he is one of those men who needs to rescue women, he will not respond positively to your litany of woe. Keep it light and positive. At some point you (and he) will need to open up and reveal negative information and discuss personal problems. But not in the first conversation. Now is not the time to discuss your physical or psychological problems, your addictions, your criminal record. Those facts are revealed after you have established a bond. That takes time.

Singles all claim they want to meet someone who doesn't play games. Unfortunately, that is an unrealistic expectation. First encounters between members of the opposite sex almost invariably begin with playing the "I'm Perfect Game." We pretend that there's nothing wrong with us, it's a wonder that we aren't already happily married! Yes, there's a bit of dishonesty involved here, but that is how the Dating Game is played. If you don't play according to the rules, you lose the game.

Romantic relationships are extremely fragile in the beginning. One wrong move, and he's gone! Don't make the mistake of turning him off by being too open in your first conversation. Just about everyone, you and he included, are looking for a reason to cross each other off the list of potential lovers. We know there are over 50 million people of the opposite sex who are single in America. We need to whittle that number down. So one false move, and they are gone. Dating is the most unforgiving game there is. Don't give him a reason to cross you off his list. One study was done with the customers of a dating service, who were asked for feedback after their first dates. The study discovered that if a guy learns nine positive things about you on a date and one negative thing, that one negative had as much impact on his memory as the nine positives!

So put your best foot forward. That's likely what he is doing, if he has any sense. Don't shoot yourself in the foot and volunteer negative information about yourself on the first date. Yes, the barriers have to come down eventually, if you are to move onto an intimate relationship. Just don't expect it to happen immediately.

Marking Your Territory

If you find a new man at a social function to be attractive, chances are other women feel the same. You might have a few minutes of fun interaction, but if he wanders off and engages another woman, there's a good chance he will forget YOU and date HER. So how do you "mark your territory?" Ask him to move away from the action at the party to a secluded corner and sit down and talk. This is making a statement that you like this guy and want to get to know him better. If you think this is being forward, you are 100% correct! That's how you snag a great guy right under the noses of other single women at the party. As long as he is distracted by other women, and the noise and bustle of the party, he won't focus on how attractive you are.

Personal Note: I produce over 50 singles parties each year in the San Francisco Bay Area (at ThePartyHotline.com). The most popular ones, that attract hundreds of people, are always dance parties. Some of my singles complain that "you can't talk to anyone, the music's too loud." My reply, which I'm sure can be irritating, is that "this is a dancing party, not a talking party. If you want to talk, go to one of my talking parties, where there is no music." But they don't want to go to the talking party, because there aren't as many people and the energy level isn't as high. The solution is to leave the commotion of the dance party and go to another room or area where it isn't as noisy and you can actually converse. Better still, ask the guy to leave the party altogether, and go out for a cup of coffee, a drink, or a bite to eat. That's really eliminating the competition!

Pinning Down Your Next Contact

The most important part of that first conversation with someone new is how you end it. Does he ask to see you again? Does he ask for your phone number or email address? If not, what do you do? If the man is a Donald Trump-like alpha male and he doesn't pursue the next step, you can be sure he doesn't plan on ever seeing you again. But the shy guy is different. The more attracted to you he may be, the more paralyzed he may be with fear of rejection. So don't let this man slip past you. Take the initiative and say, "I really enjoyed meeting you. When may I see you again?" Too forward? What's the alternative?. If you say nothing you probably will never see him again. As an alternative, you could hand him your business card. Every woman needs a business card, with at least your phone number or email address. It doesn't matter whether you have a business! But this is a low-percentage strategy. If he's shy, he's unlikely to call you. Another alternative would be to ask for his phone number or email address. Don't do this unless you are sure you will have the fortitude to follow through. The best strategy, however, is to pin down your next contact. "When may I see you again?" This is the boldest step, and also the one most likely to ensure you will indeed rendezvous in the future. If you have gauged his interest accurately, he will agree to see you at a specific time and place. That's called a DATE. Most mature singles cringe at that word (feels like high school all over again), but setting a date is the best way to make sure you will see each other again. Otherwise, you have wasted your time with this shy fellow.

If you are so fortunate as to be with a man who isn't afraid to ask you out, don't make the mistake of being unprepared to commit to a date. "I have to check my calendar at home" is a deadly response. He's not going to believe that dodge. He will conclude that you are not interested in seeing him again and are sparing his feelings with a white lie. Personal Note: I met my wife Debby at one of my singles parties at a fancy hotel ballroom in San Francisco. Rather than ask for her phone number, I asked "When may I see you again?" She replied that she would have to check her schedule and offered her phone number. I declined accepting her number and instead offered mine, on the off chance that she really did need to check her calendar at home. To my surprise she called a couple of days later, and we were off to the races! It turned out that she had to make sure someone could watch her elderly mother before she could commit to a date.

Asking for a date during a first encounter seems to some to be an overly assertive technique. But what's the alternative? Most singles who exchange contact information wind up never seeing each other again. What a tragedy! Think of all the trouble you went to attending an event away from home, all the boring, superficial conversations you've had to endure to wind up finally meeting someone promising. Why throw that away with a low-percentage strategy such as exchanging phone numbers or email addresses?

Dating Safety

Surely your parents taught you never to get into a car with a stranger. It's great advice for a child, and just as valuable for adult women! If you meet a man at a social event, regardless if he appears harmless, don't get into his car to go out to dinner or a cup of coffee or whatever. Take you own car. And don't invite him into your home after the first encounter. If a friend vouches for him, you can ignore this advice, but not with a total stranger. Your first "date" ideally will be in the middle of the day, in a public setting, with each of you driving in separate cars.

STDs

Just as you don't get into a car with a stranger, you shouldn't have unpro-tected sex with one either. Sexually transmitted diseases such as herpes, chla-mydia, gonorrhea, syphilis are quite prevalent. Use the proper precautions.

The 3 Date Rule... and Other Myths

Nobody knows who invented The 3 Date Rule, but be clear it doesn't apply to you! You should never feel compelled to have sex before you are ready. As old-fashioned as it may seem today, many women wait until their wed-ding night. Others don't wait for the third date. And some engage in sex after a casual encounter. Everyone has their own moral code. The important thing is for you to keep to yours, whatever it may be. Yes, there is some risk to holding out. The man may lose interest. Or conversely, if you are "too easy," you might be abandoned. Different men have different expectations. The best policy is to ignore their expectations and cling to your own.

Sex and the Single Girl

The number one sexual myth is that men want sex more than women. Nothing could be further from the truth! The difference between the sexes usually is that men want sex NOW. It's a matter of timing. Historically women have delayed having sex, because they fear the consequences of sex with a man who abandons them. They end up with all the responsibilities of parenthood, without any help. So traditionally most women have avoided immediate intimacy, waiting for a bond to develop before opening up physically.

Often men respond that there is no reason to postpone sex, that prophylactics can ensure that there is no unwanted pregnancy. If your religious values allow you to use birth control, this is true. But women have a greater burden than just the fear of pregnancy. Our society has a double standard regarding early intimacy in a relationship. While the man is often labeled a "stud," the women is labeled a "slut." The consequences to a woman's self-esteem can be just as severe as the impact on her body by the onset of pregnancy.

You are not in this world to fulfill the expectations of anyone other than yourself. Not those of your parents. Not those of your church. And definitely not your date's expectations. Your sole obligation is to yourself. You are the final arbiter of whether you should be intimate on the first date, only after marriage, or somewhere in between. Because you are the one who has to live with the consequences.

Best First Dates

Dinner and dancing is fine, if you have a hunch this guy could be a keeper. But why invest so much time and energy on someone you aren't sure about? Why not keep it cheap and casual? An ice cream or coffee date is ideal. Don't go to a movie, where you get to know the actors better than each other. Just find a place to sit down and talk.

Who Pays?

Ever since the dawn of the Women's Liberation Movement back in the 70s, this has been a question singles agonize over. Many women never deviate from the expectation that the man always pays, whether it's the first date, or the twentieth. Nothing wrong with that, except a man may conclude that you are taking advantage of him. Wealthy men, in particular, may be suspicious of a woman who never offers to pay (at least half) or give him a home-cooked meal. You will score points with a man if you offer to pay at least half. What do you do if you can't afford to split the tab at a fancy restaurant chosen by your male companion? Suggest a more affordable alternative. Remember the suggestion above of the ice cream parlor or coffee shop?

Some men insist on paying as part of being the dominant member of the relationship. If you feel comfortable being dominated, then by all means let him pay, every time. But if you want to assert some independence, the easiest way is to pull your weight financially. Be aware that some men expect you to provide them with sexual favors in exchange for an inexpensive meal or night on the town. If you are going to feel guilty turning a man down if he's dropped a bundle of cash on you, then you should definitely insist on paying at least half. If a man makes it clear he wants to pay (and you are clear with yourself that you will not feel obligated to thank him by sleeping with him), then it might be wise not to protest too loudly. Let him pay if that's how he feels comfortable in a male-female relationship, even if you earn more than he does.

PART 6
The Nuts & Bolts of Intimacy

How do you move beyond the superficiality of early dating to emotional intimacy? First, it takes time. Demanding too much intimacy, too soon, may scare off a promising prospect. So be patient. But at some time you have to take a risk if your relationship is to blossom.

If you are around a man who is somewhat closed emotionally (which probably includes most men) this can be a delicate process. You don't want to get too personal too soon. Wait until there is a good comfort level in the relationship. Then set a good example by beginning to reveal some of your secrets. Hopefully he will get the hint and do the same. If not, you have to pry. You may sometimes feel like a dentist pulling teeth, but you have to find out whether this man is right for you. If he keeps everything secret from you, your relationship will never mature.

Remember the qualities on your *Must List* and ask him each of the critical questions. Not in one session of course! Over the course of time you need to find out as much about him as possible. And you need to have the courage to reveal who you really are, warts and all. You may reveal something that he finds unacceptable. That's the risk. But consider the alternatives. That he discovers a deal-breaker AFTER he marries you, and then divorces you. Or that you keep these secrets until you die, and never have a healthy, happy, loving relationship.

Letting Go of Resentments

Your past relationships with men, beginning with your father and continuing with brothers, boyfriends, and ex-husbands can cripple your future interactions with men. How do you let go of your resentments?

1. Make a list of negative qualities you have encountered in men.
2. Next to each negative quality, write down the name(s) that correspond
3. Try to understand why a man might have this quality. For example, a man might hide his sad emotions because he was teased for being a crybaby.
4. Were you in any way complicit? Did you clearly communicate your dislike of this quality, or did you suffer in silence? If you never shared your resentment, was it reasonable for you to expect him to change?

One of the most common complaints about men is that "they want to jump into bed immediately." One Florida professor had his students walk down a busy street and ask strangers, "Would you like to go to bed with me?" All of the women said no, but 75% of the men said yes, they wanted to have sex with a complete stranger! We could explore evolutionary history to try to explain this, but why bother? The fact is that men in our society are rewarded for "scoring" with women. Their self-esteem often revolves around being a "stud." You won't be able to change this, so why continue to allow yourself to get upset each time a casual acquaintance "puts the make" on you? Accept this as a typical male trait, and move on. Resentment comes from expecting things to change. In this case they won't, so why hold on to this?

Another common resentment is that men play too many games. One way to let go of this resentment is to realize the other half of this truth: women play just as many games. Men resent women who flirt shamelessly and use sexual innuendos, then get angry when a man pressures her to have sex. One of the all-time most popular TV game shows was *The Dating Game*. And indeed dating is a game and both sides are less than totally honest. Deal with it!

A third common dating complaint is that men often ask for your phone number and never call. Why would a man not keep his commitment to call, after you honestly thought you made a good connection with him? Consider the many possibilities:

- He lost your number
- He's afraid to call because you might reject him
- He forgot who you were after he sobered up

Regardless of the cause, men often don't follow up with a call. That's why the wise course is to agree to meet again at a specific time and place and then exchange numbers so you can confirm the date.

It should come as no surprise that men also have to deal with resentments they hold towards women. As mentioned earlier, the most common complaint is that of the woman leading him on. Another is insisting he leave her home after a night of drinking and carousing, subjecting him to the dangers of driving while intoxicated.

Many men complain that women are too emotional. Or they give the silence treatment rather than specify their complaints. The list goes on.

Why are their so many resentments between the sexes. Probably because they are the OPPOSITE sex. John Gray's analogy is correct: Men ARE from Mars and Women ARE from Venus. That leads to excitement and passion, but also to incompatibility and resentment.

Sharing Negative Feelings

Negative feelings must be shared. Otherwise they fester. But there is a proper time and place. If you know your partner is not in the mood to hear anything negative (maybe he's having a bad day, has just been fired, has lost a loved one recently), wait until a better time.

Never share negative feelings when there are witnesses. No one likes to be embarrassed in public, even among intimate friends and relatives.

Making "I" Statements

Instead of making accusatory statements ("You never listen!") make "I" statements ("I don't feel heard right now.") Not "You don't love me anymore," but "I don't feel loved." The more you avoid accusing your partner and the more you take ownership of your own feelings, the stronger your relationship.

Avoiding the Inflammatory

Don't make absolute accusations: "You never take my feelings into consideration" or "You always flirt with other women when we go out." Usually these statements, while true most of the time, are not true all of the time. The alternative is to say, "I wish you consider my feelings right now" or "I wish you would focus your attention on me right now, not on others."

Here are other things to avoid if you don't want to blow up your relationship:

- Foul language when referring to your partner
- Screaming and yelling
- Sarcasm
- Brutal honesty
- Threatening gestures with fists, knives, etc.
- Hitting below the belt. Referring to something about which they are especially sensitive.
- Dredging up things from the past that should be forgiven and forgotten

Accentuating the Positive

Negativity is the poison that kills loving relationships. Research reveals that in healthy relationships people experience the positive from their partner five times as often as the negative. Unfortunately, most relationships have this ratio reversed. Every time you criticize or insult your partner, you owe him five positives, which could be a compliment, a hug, a back rub. Personal Note: As a school teacher for many years, I was advised to catch the kids doing something right, instead of always noticing their misbehavior. We all have a tendency to take the good for granted and focus on the bad. Fight that tendency!

PART 7

It's Raining Men

Single men are everywhere. You probably pass by attractive bachelors every day on your way to work, the supermarket, the gas station. All you have to do is leave the safety and security of your home. If you are a virtual shut-in, you won't ever meet everyone. The love of your life won't ever fall through your skylight!

The supermarket is a great place to meet men. You can always tell who is single by what's in the cart. Six packs of beer and frozen food – he's single. Pampers in the cart? He's married. Personal Note: I was born in San Francisco, which has what once was the most famous supermarket in the world: The Marina Safeway. Every Wednesday night used to be Singles Night, where you would often see women dressed to the nines, rather than jeans and athletic shoes, hoping to attract a special man. The way to meet people was to "accidentally" bump into their shopping cart. Or you could ask, "Where can I find the brussels sprouts?" Jim Spillane, a now-retired dating coach, would teach flirting seminars on the Marina Green and then take the class across the street to the Safeway, where his students could practice their newly learned skills.

Most people are desperate to find the shortest line at the checkstands. Not the best strategy if you want to meet someone new. Next time you shop, stand in line behind the most attractive guy who appears to be single!

You'll find a lot of single men at the laundromat. You can always tell which guys are single by the clothes he is washing. Skip any man who has both male and female clothing. He is part of a couple. (Or he's a cross-dresser). Dolly Parton met her husband in a laundromat.

How to Survive in a Singles Bar

Singles bars have a bad reputation. Supposedly only alcoholics and losers go there. Personal Note: At my dating seminars I often ask people to raise their hands if they have ever been to a singles bar. Just about every hand usually goes up. Everyone laughs when I declare, "these are the kinds of people you are likely to meet in a singles bar." So yes, people sometimes do find lasting love in a bar.

If you don't indulge in alcohol and hope to meet someone similar to yourself, obviously bars are a bad venue for you. Assuming that you are not adverse to a cocktail or two, a lounge or nightclub is a suitable place to look. Bear in mind, however, that the term "singles bar" is a misnomer, as no bar exists that caters only to singles. A singles bar is just a place which is known to the community to attract many singles. But beware of married men who go to bars to meet women and engage in the infamous "wedding band trick": leaving the ring behind in his glove compartment.

Many women will not enter a singles bar because of concern for their safety or fear that some obnoxious man will "hit" on them and won't take no for an answer. One way to deal with this is to complain to the bartender, waiter/waitress, or bouncer, who will ask the offending male to leave. A singles bar cannot survive if the women stop coming, which will be the result if the bar does not deal with offensive men.

Don't let Mr. Wrong monopolize you. Mr. Right may want to approach you, but courtesy requires that you stop your current conversation. So if the wrong guy sits next to you, leave your seat! You'll meet more men standing than sitting.

Don't listen to Mr. Wrong's life story. You are not his therapist. After a sentence or two, excuse yourself and say you have to use the restroom or some other excuse.

Never give him your phone number. Ask for his instead and dump it at your first opportunity.

Old-Fashioned Places to Meet

Dating Websites and Apps are all viable ways to meet Mr. Right. But don't overlook meeting the old-fashioned way, face-to-face. There are thousands of non-profit organizations that cater primarily to singles.

Churches

Many singles organizations meet at churches. If you are an atheist or agnostic, this would not be the most appropriate place to meet men. However, you don't have to be a regular church-goer or a member of the congregation to attend. All churches are open to the general public (especially to sinners!), so feel free to show up at the local church singles group.

Personal Note: I got my start in the dating industry by attending a singles group at the local Unitarian Church, even though I wasn't Unitarian. Before I knew what was happening, I was drafted into becoming chairman of the group. I was the sixth grade teacher at a Catholic school at the time and was having a hard time meeting women. I couldn't date any of my fellow teachers because they were all either married or nuns. Likewise my customers were all off-limits, because they were eleven years old! Unitarian Singles was a godsend for me. I wound up not only meeting lots of nice single women, but finding a whole new career!

Secular Organizations

There also are thousands of secular singles clubs in America. Many of them are activity oriented: single golfers, tennis players, dancers, pet-lovers, chess players, movie-goers, entrepreneurs, etc. Some cater to specific races or ethnicities, such as Black Singles, Asian Singles, Hispanic Singles, Indian (Desi) Singles, etc. Some groups cater to specific ages. Others target singles in a particular town or city.

Googling Your Way to a Loving Relationship

If you haven't already learned how to use a search engine such as *Google* or *Yahoo*, ask a friend to teach you, or sign up for a class at the local community center. *Google* is your friend in the search for men. Just type in the search term that best describes the man you seek. You can type, "Men 20-25 Chicago Athletic" or Hispanic Single Men Miami" or "Mature Men

Wyoming." You won't believe all the links you can click that will lead you to your goal! For a more generic search, type in "singles parties" or "singles dances" or "singles groups", plus the name of your city.

One special resource is *Meetup.com*, which literally lists thousands of singles groups all over the country. You can search by interest and many other criteria. Many meetups, while limiting themselves to the unattached, still have large majorities who are single.

Service clubs, such as *Rotary, Elks, Lions*, etc., which are predominantly male, are also good options. Likewise for charitable organizations and business organizations. Your local *Chamber of Commerce* has frequent events, which are great for both business networking and meeting new friends.

Love at the Office

Your job can be a tremendous resource for meeting eligible men, if you choose the RIGHT job. Alas, many women are school teachers or nurses, where they mainly interact with women. Personal Note: I wasn't meeting anyone special as a school teacher. Luckily I changed jobs to my current career (dating expert) and literally met thousands of single women (met them, not necessarily dated them) until I met my wife Debby at one of my dating seminars/dances.

Male dominant industries such as tech jobs, computer programming, engineering, and construction come to mind immediately (yes, there are female carpenters, plumbers, and electricians, and they are in constant contact with bachelors). Personal Note: One woman, who has helped me as a volunteer at my singles parties, is the only woman working with 40 engineers. "But you wouldn't date any of them!" she exclaims. Some women also complain about nerds in the workplace.

Assuming you come across someone attractive at work, should you date him? Depends. There is a small risk that either you or he will have to change jobs if the romance fizzles. In one survey of 1,800 professional women, only 5% thought the office romance had hurt their careers. The good news from this study is that 20% of office romances led to marriage and these marriages were four times more likely to last than those who met through other methods.

That's why many women at large companies date someone in a different department (you are in accounting and he is in sales). Often they first meet by the water cooler or at the company picnic or holiday party.

Temp jobs allow you to meet new men with every assignment. Service industry jobs, where you directly interact with large numbers of people (waitress, store clerk, barista) don't usually pay well. But you can meet lots of men. PERSONAL NOTE: One of my cousins met her husband at the bank where she worked as a teller. She knew all about his personal finances BEFORE the first date!

A volunteer job doesn't pay anything at all, but could be the springboard for a great romance. Volunteer for an organization that might attract a man with your interests. For example, if you love the arts, volunteer at the symphony, opera, or ballet, or work at a museum.

Meeting Through Friends

If you aren't meeting as many good men as you wish, your friends may be holding out on you. Many don't want the responsibility of introducing you to someone for a potentially disastrous relationship. Or they are just plain lazy. Regardless, your friends, relatives, and business associates all know bachelors you don't know. They are just reluctant to admit it. Don't take NO for an answer. Lean on them to introduce you to suitable unattached males. But don't expect them to take too many risks. Share with them exactly what you want (your *Must List*) so they don't have to read your mind. If you are clear about your expectations, they can feel somewhat confident that whomever they introduce to you is a worthwhile prospect.

Meeting Men at Home

Consider asking your BFFs to co-host a party with you in your home. Ask each to bring a bottle or dish to share. Most importantly, require that each woman be responsible for at least one bachelor coming to the party.

The single women of France are no dummies when it comes to meeting eligible men. Every year they throw a "Best of the Men Party," where the women all invite the finest bachelors they know, with whom they are not romantically involved. That means fathers, sons, brothers, cousins, neighbors, bosses, subordinates, and coworkers. Each man is not only certified to be legally single, but they all come highly recommended!

As noted earlier, single women in San Francisco complain bitterly that there are not enough eligible straight men. One group of bachelorettes named their parties "Single, Straight, and Breathing." They required every woman at a party to bring TWO straight bachelors. Eventually the group disbanded, because all the women found boyfriends or husbands!

If you are fortunate to live in a large apartment complex you will find many bachelors. Invite them to a potluck in your home or that of one of your neighbors, or in the complex's clubhouse. Or throw a poolside party or barbecue.

If you live in a detached home, get to know your neighbors, and help organize a block party outdoors or in one of your homes. Join your neighborhood association and attend their events. If there aren't any events in your neighborhood, take the initiative and organize a "Meet Your Neighbors Party."

Eliminating the Competition

Most dating experts recommend doing something you love to meet new friends who share your interests. That's great advice if you want to meet other women. Its disastrous if you hope to meet men. The reason they are called the opposite sex is because they are OPPOSITE. Men and women often have different interests. It would be great if you could meet men who share all of your hobbies and interests. But limiting yourself to that small percentage of men isn't the wisest strategy. Personal Note: Women who attend my singles events often complain that there are always too many women and not enough men. This is especially true at singles events held at churches. So I suggested Tuesday night coed volleyball at the local high school gym. It only cost $5 and was loaded with men! One woman responded, "Oh, I couldn't do that. It would break my nails!"

Ask yourself, "what do most men love that most women hate?" The dreaded "S" word: Sports. If you are somewhat athletic, you might join a coed softball or volleyball league. If you are not, being a spectator at sporting events is a great way to meet men. If you are on a tight budget you might not want to invest in a live football, baseball, basketball, or hockey event. But you can certainly afford to go to a sports bar, where admission is free and the ratio is always favorable. Incidentally, nowadays with giant affordable flat screen televisions, every bar in America is a Sports Bar!

There is a legendary woman in San Francisco who went to a different tavern every week during the football season, especially for Monday Night Football. The drinks were cheap and there often was free food. She had absolutely no interest in football and would sit in a corner far away from the televisions. At halftime men would come up to her and ask, "What are you doing here, lady?" She would answer, "I'm balancing my checkbook, see?" This woman met dozens of single men each year using this one method. She eagerly awaited the first night of football each year, so she could meet her new batch of men!

If you are both female and love sports, you have a tremendous advantage over women who hate sports and discriminate against men who love them. Women who exclude sports fans because they seek "a higher quality man" are shortchanging themselves. Studies reveal that many of the most intelligent, best-educated, wealthiest, most cultured men love sports.

Do you think that football is stupid? If so, you do not understand the intricacies of the game. Coaching a football team requires a facile intellect, as does playing the position of quarterback. If you don't understand the difference between a touchdown and a field goal, learn! After you have mastered the basics of football, including the various positions, rules, teams, and heroes of the gridiron, you might discover that you actually like football. Likewise for learning about baseball, basketball, and hockey. At least you will be able to hold an intelligent conversation about something many men are rabid about.

Classes

Your local community college, adult education department, or recreation department probably lists dozens of classes or athletic teams that are great ways to connect with new friends who share your interests. One survey revealed that the main reason people took these classes was not to learn something, but to meet people! Ask yourself what kind of class would a man you would like to meet likely attend? If you want to meet a guy who has money, why not take a class on real estate investments, commodities, or the stock market? Personal note: A man at one of my dating seminars shared his story of taking a class that he knew would be full of women. He walked into the room on the first night, and it was a nightmare. 50 women and he was the only man! It was a class on PMS. He expected the women to be unfriendly and suspicious. Instead, many wanted to meet the man who was "sensitive to women's problems."

Coed softball and volleyball are great options. Personal Note: Back in my singles days, I took an aerobics class, not just to get healthier, but specifically to meet women. The ratio was great: 3 women for every man! Unfortunately, halfway through the session I discovered why there were so few men: every muscle in my body cramped up simultaneously. Apparently men are the weaker sex and weren't meant to do aerobics. But it was a great place to meet women!

Dance classes that cater to singles are great for meeting men. Many Hispanic nightclubs have salsa, cha cha, rhumba, and merengue classes. Country & Western bars often teach line dancing and the two-step. Professional dance studios can be nationwide chains, such as Arthur Murray and Fred Astaire, or local. These classes are fun, and you will meet men who will hopefully take you out dancing once in a while, should you become a couple.

To Swipe...or Not to Swipe

Meeting face-to-face is rapidly becoming obsolete in Twenty first century America. The theory is that meeting face-to-face takes too much time, expense and effort. Plus there is too small of a dating pool from which to select Mr. Right. Dressing up for a night on the town, driving or taking public transportation to the venue, then having superficial conversations with several people can be hard work and very time-consuming. Buying food or drink at the venue can be expensive. A more efficient alternative might be to advertise for what you want (or read the ads of others seeking a romantic partner) and potentially choosing from thousands (or even millions) of singles in your area.

It all started with newspaper personal in the classified section. After World War II ended in Europe in May of 1945, millions of displaced people couldn't locate their family and friends. They didn't even know if any of them were still alive. One way to find them was to advertise in the newspapers. Eventually the concept spread to America—with a twist. Instead of advertising for people you already knew, why not use the printed page to find someone to love—or at least to interact for a night of lovemaking? *The Berkeley Barb* became popular in the San Francisco Bay Area for singles looking for love. The ads were often racy, and wildly popular. The concept spread to New York City in *The Village Voice*. Eventually every major city in America had an "alternative weekly," which competed for advertising dollars with the more conservative daily newspapers. Singles would exchange letters through the mail, forwarded by the newspaper. Eventually 900 services were created for people to phone each other for a fee (by calling a number with the prefix 900) after reading an ad in the newspaper.

The lucrative 900 industry was destroyed by the invention of online dating, which was much cheaper and enabled singles to choose from vast numbers of prospective dates. Personal Note: I was introduced to online dating by Dan Bender, a close friend and business partner. In the early 90s we operated *Cupid's Network*, which primarily published personal ads in alternative weeklies. Dan suggested we start a "dating website." I said, "What?" "You've heard of the World Wide Web, haven't you?" asked Dan. "Nope," I replied. "How about the internet?" "That, I've heard of," I replied. "We should start an online dating service on what is going to become the most popular part of the internet." I was skeptical, but what the hell, give it a shot. *Cupid's Online Network* was born. AS.org (short for American Singles, my non-profit organization) launched on Valentine's Day, 1995. There was only one other dating website in the world at the time, *WebPesonals.com*, so this was getting in on the ground floor. AS.org became wildly successful, eventually peaking at 250,000 members. Today that's a tiny database. But back in the mid-90s, that was a huge number. Membership was free, since we were non-profit.

A lot has happened since 1995. Huge dating websites with tens of millions of members were created. Some of the largest are *Match.com, OKCupid.*

com, PlentyofFish.com, EHarmony.com, etc. In addition to the huge websites that cater to a giant, amorphous population, there are smaller, boutique websites that cater to niches in the population. For example, *ChristianMingle. com* (for single Christians), *JDate.com* (for single Jews), *50PlusConnects.com*, and so forth. There are now well over 2,000 dating websites for every possible person you could hope to meet, from Vegetarians to Dog Lovers to Black Singles, Asian Singles, Hispanic Singles, Military Singles, and so forth.

While creating a profile (brief biography of yourself) is free on most of these websites, you usually have to pay a fee of $20 or $30 a month to *choose* people to date on the website and have full functionality. The fee is the least costly part of the process. Online dating takes an enormous amount of time to go through the often huge database of prospective dates, review their photos and biographies, email back and forth, etc. And that's before you undergo the slow and expensive process of actually meeting the candidates face-to-face. Successful online dating is not for the lazy.

One of the negatives of online dating is that often people email back and forth multiple times, without ever meeting in the flesh. Many engage in virtual dating and even virtual sex, where the entire relationship is online.

Personal Note: A woman who attended one of my dating seminars found an interesting, efficient way to weed out inappropriate partners. Every Saturday she went to an upscale coffee shop a couple of blocks from her San Francisco home and dedicated most of the day to meeting her online matches. She scheduled them for half hour time slots so she could interview the maximum number of men in a day. She explained it all ahead of time to the owner so he wouldn't come to the wrong conclusion that she was a hooker meeting her customers.

The biggest advantage to online dating is the ability to go through vast numbers of prospective partners to find the one person who has close to everything on your *Wish List*. Hopefully you'll have everything on his! The disadvantage is that you are competing against thousands, possibly millions of available women. Just as you may have a huge Wish List, he may have one equally lengthy. The chances that he will settle on you are slim.

Another disadvantage of online dating is that it encourages people, especially men, to engage in a long series of quick, superficial encounters, rather than intimate long-term relationships. Why should he commit to you when there are so many other enticing women available?

Perhaps the biggest complaints about online dating revolve around dishonesty. Women often lie about their age and weight. Men frequently lie about their height and income. And the photos that are posted online can be 20 years and 20 pounds ago!

Women over 40 often feel strongly tempted to lie online. Otherwise it's hard to compete against the multitude of women in their 20s and 30s who are vying for the same men. Should you lie about your age to even the playing field? That's for you to decide. Bear in mind that if you later meet someone special online, you will have to explain to him that lied about your age because you thought it was unfair to be discriminated against because of your age. Hopefully he will understand.

Dating apps are quickly overtaking dating websites in popularity. The most famous app, *Tinder*, boasts millions upon millions of users. *Tinder* provides you with an endless choice of potential partners. If you live in a large city, like New York City, there could be many thousands of options within easy driving or even walking distance of your home! Photos move across your smart phone screen endlessly, with their age, location, and brief bio. You swipe right if you want to reach out to them, left to discard them. A very cold process. But quite addictive to many. If there is mutual attraction (he swipes to the right on your photo as well), you are given the opportunity to message one another. This process is called "double opt-in."

Dating apps are particularly suited to photogenic women aged 18-34, who can expect to be overwhelmed by responses. *Tinder* is a free service. You can download the app onto your smart phone through the Apple App Store or Google Play Store. Or if you don't have a smart phone, you can visit www.gotinder.com to participate online. You must login with *Facebook*, so your prospective matches can find out more information about you. Other popular dating apps are *Zoosk*, *Hinge*, and *Love Flutter*.

Matchmaker, Matchmaker, Make Me a Match

The opposite to using modern technology is old-fashioned matchmaking, as popularized by the smash Broadway hits and movies *Hello Dolly!* and *Fiddler on the Roof*. Today's matchmakers, of course, are less yenta and more executive recruiter. Many busy women, who have more money than time to spend on finding a great guy, turn to professional matchmakers. They like the personal service they receive. The search begins with an extensive personal interview.

The most famous matchmaker is Patti Stanger, TV's *Millionaire Matchmaker*. The world's largest matchmaking service is *Its Just Lunch*, with offices in most major American cities. There are also many private firms in the big cities.

If you prefer to do your own matchmaking, but need a little help, dating coaches abound all over America. They help you define your best match and develop a detailed customized plan on how and where to meet him. They may also provide makeup and wardrobe advice, teach you how to flirt, hold your hand, and listen to your woeful tales of disastrous dates and relationships.

Time Won't Let Me

Clearly you could spend 24 hours a day, every day, searching for good men, who are everywhere. But where's the time to look for them? Most people spend more time searching for a new car than a new spouse. There are all kinds of excuses. "I just don't have the time to go out looking for Mr. Right. It takes two hours each day to get back and forth from work, plus ten hours on the job. Then there's the shopping and the cleaning. A woman's gotta sleep sometime."

It's easy to justify staying home and not meeting anyone new. But the truth is, if you stay home, you are going to stay single.

All of us have enough time to do whatever has priority in our lives. If almost all of your time and energy goes into your job, that means finding a man to share your life is of a lesser priority. If you are not currently meeting enough attractive men, look at your schedule as the possible culprit.

Single Mothers

Committing time for meeting a special man is a particular challenge for single mothers, who are usually overwhelmed with other responsibilities. Single mothers sometimes feel guilty when they leave their children in the hands of others, particularly if the father is out of the picture or only helps out on a rare occasion. Some single mothers overcompensate for the absent parent spending almost all of their time when not earning of living. The kids come first and last.

This can be a mistake. If you don't take of you, your ability to parent will suffer. If you are unhappy, likely so will your kids. It's important to carve out time just for your own needs. Especially you need to have time with adults (male and female) without the children present. And you need to invest time in going to places where you might be around new men if you hope to meet your romantic needs.

It's easy to feel guilty on a date, especially if our children cry when you "abandon" them to the care of a babysitter. Your kids don't realize it is to their advantage for you to take care of Number One on occasion. Don't allow your batteries to run down because you neglect your own needs.

Child care is very expensive and may be unaffordable to many single mothers. One solution is to share with other single mothers. Your local school or church likely has single mothers who would be thrilled to watch your kids on occasion in return for your reciprocation. Try placing notices on bulletin boards at your office, church, or supermarket. You can also join a cooperative babysitting group. If a *Google* search doesn't reveal one in your area, start one yourself.

Sharing child care can also have another benefit: new friends in a similar stage of life with yourself. No one can understand what you are going through more than another single mother, who will find it easy to empathize with you. Don't be afraid to ask for understanding and emotional support from other single moms (and dads).

Grandparents and other close relatives are usually soft touches when it comes to asking for help with childcare. Don't be reluctant to lean on your ex for help, even if you can't stand talking to him. Unless he is abusive with you or the children, it is imperative that you overcome your resentments and have as cordial a relationship as possible. Don't allow your anger to deprive your kids of a father and yourself of a free babysitter!

Will the children be damaged if you carve out time for a social life? Studies reveal that kids are not damaged by less time with a single parent, as long as they have QUALITY TIME. If you never really talk to your kids, without the distraction of the TV or smart phone, it really doesn't matter how much time you give them. Schedule time each day to sit down and share how your day has gone, without anything else in the background.

All Work and No Play... Means You Stay Single

Women who are childless also can find allotting time for meeting men to be a challenge. The search for the almighty dollar can be all-consuming, particularly if you have only one income. It's easy to become a workaholic, particularly if you own your own business or have a demanding boss. However, unless you come across attractive bachelors in the course of earning a living, every hour spent at work is wasted time in terms of finding a lasting, loving relationship. Consider the price you pay for devoting almost all of your time to making money, instead of meeting your social and romantic needs.

Is it possible for you to devote less time and energy working? Will your happiness be reduced significantly if you earn less money? How important is it for you to find a fulfilling relationship with a man? Reading dating books is a good start, but if you are not really committed to finding love, it's not going to happen. The test of your commitment is the time you apply. Ask yourself three questions:

1. How much money do I need (bare minimum) to be happy?
2. How many hours can I cut and still earn that amount?
3. What changes can I make to my schedule that would free the maximum number of hours to socialize?

Here are some ways to reduce your work schedule:

- Delegate. It is ego-gratifying to believe that your business or department would collapse without you working around the clock, but is that really true? As humbling as it may be, there are others who might be able to do your job. Not as well as you, of course! But good enough. Delegate to them.
- Subcontract. Other companies would love the opportunity to relieve you of some of your responsibilities.
- Use labor-saving devices. Modern technology makes it easy to get more done in less time.

PART 8

Don't Fall in Love with the Wrong Guy!

f you commit yourself to meeting large numbers of eligible men in the venues described later in this book, you will develop a problem that most single women wish they had: too many prospects. How do you separate the wheat from the chaff.quickly and efficiently? It may sound ruthless, but don't waste your time on inappropriate men. Personal Note: I maintained a friendship with two women I had dated in the past. Both of them wanted to be mothers and wound up falling in love with men who had vasectomies! They could have discovered this crucial fact much earlier, just by asking.

So how do you quickly discover whether a man has all the qualities you require for a lasting, loving, happy relationship?

There are 3 methods. Use them all.

Interrogation

Develop a list of *Killer Questions* to ask a man early in a relationship. This is a list of questions based on your *Must List* from an earlier chapter. They are called *Killer Questions* because if the man answers even one question incorrectly, it kills the relationship. Time to move on!

Some women in search of love have been known to pull out a checklist to grill their first dates. Hopefully you are more subtle than that! Memorize the questions on your list and be sure to ask as many of them as you can without being obnoxious. Personal Note: Back in my single days I wasn't shy about asking questions on a first date. I found that most women were quite receptive to my questions. Except one woman who asked, "What are you, a District Attorney?

In an earlier chapter you were encouraged to boil down a lengthy *Wish List* to a more reasonable *Must List*. It may have been painful to give up some of your fondest fantasies in order to have a realistic chance to find Mr. Right. But some go too far in crossing qualities off of the *Wish List*. Now is the time to add a few requirements that you may have overlooked earlier, but which are essential to a successful long-term relationship or marriage. Here are some questions that should be on your list:

1. **Marital Status**: "Are you legally single?" Pretty obvious, and yet millions of women have fallen in love with men they ASSUMED were single. Not all married men will admit it, but many will. So ask the question. If he answers, "sort of," there are two critical follow-up questions: "Have you filed for divorce and have you moved out?" If the answer to either of these questions is NO, time to move on.
2. **Kids**: "Do you have kids?" If you marry a man with children, his kids become yours. It's critical to know what you are getting yourself into! "Do you want more and how soon do you want them?" If you want to bear children and your biological clock is ticking, listen closely to his answer to this one.
3. **Location**: "Do you plan to continue to live in this area long-term?" Don't assume that because you live in the same town or close by, that this will continue. He may be in town temporarily and plan to move far away once his current job or contract or internship expires. Are you prepared to leave your home, your job, your family, and your friends?
4. **Faithfulness**. "Have you ever cheated on a girlfriend or wife?" Again, not every man will answer this one honestly, but many will. But they won't volunteer negative information. You have to ask.

Observation

You can learn a lot about a man just by watching him interact with others. Observe how he treats wait staff and store clerks. If he is rude or overbearing with them, eventually he will treat you the same way, after the honeymoon fades. How does he act around his kids, parents, relatives, and closest friends. If he is abusive with them, some day he will abuse you as well.

Watch his drinking and other habits that might concern you. If he is on his best behavior, there are tricks you can employ to uncover hidden problems. For example, if you have had a bad experience in the past with an alcoholic, you might be afraid of engaging with another. You can your date how much he drinks, and you might be lucky and have him admit to a problem. But you can't take his word for it. Men lie when dating women! (Of course women do also, but that's not your concern). So why not intentionally try to get him drunk? "Have another one, dear." If you succeed, move on the next man in your life. The same holds true for drugs.

The most important part of observation is to understand that "what you see is what you get." He will NOT be different after the wedding day.

Investigation

Some single women actually hire a private investigator to check a man out. This is certainly appropriate, especially if you are wealthy and a possible target for gigolos. If you can't afford a P.I., you can do it yourself. There are many companies, available through the internet, that specialize in checking out prospective husbands. Online databases will reveal whether or not he is already married, has a criminal record, bankruptcies, and other problems. They can discover whether or not he has given you his real name or place of employment. You can do this yourself, by searching online databases. Bear in mind, however, that if a man does not have a criminal record in your area, that doesn't mean he isn't on parole for murder in another state! Likewise, he might have a wife in another region.

A more personal method is to check him out by talking to his parents, relatives, friends, coworkers, and business associates, if you are fortunate to meet them naturally while dating. You may not have the privacy to ask personal questions about him, initially, but if you bide your time, hopefully you will be able to talk to his intimate friends and relatives off in a corner sometime. Assuming it's a social situation and alcohol is available, you have a good chance of discovering a few intimate secrets that your boyfriend has been concealing! This is a risky strategy, because he will be angry if he discovers you are investigating him behind his back. So be subtle.

The best person to talk to, of course, is his Ex. She will give you all the dirt, especially if you ply her with booze. Very sneaky, but consider the stakes. Are you willing to risk your happiness, perhaps even your physical safety with someone who is perfect on the outside but may be concealing violent behavior, cheating on his spouse, and other tawdry faults?

Interrogation, observation, and investigation are not romantic. There is a time for love and there a time for truth. Make sure you encounter both!

50 Ways to Leave Your Lover

What do you do if you find yourself in a relationship with a man who he is missing an essential quality on your *Must List*? Dump him! Sounds harsh, but why waste your time (and his) on a relationship that is going nowhere! Every minute wasted on Mr. Wrong is time that could be spent searching for Mr. Right.

It's hard to abandon a romantic partner. The relationship may not be going anywhere, but it's comfortable. Who wants to return to the dating jungle? All those boring social events where everyone wears a mask and pretends to be something they are not. You may dread abandoning a partner for fear of being alone. Or you may be dependent on him for financial reasons. Women have a particularly difficult time abandoning the father of their children. Being a single mother is not easy. Guilt is also a barrier to cutting the wrong man loose. How can you devastate a man who tells you he loves you?

You can't allow sentiment to sidetrack your search for someone right for you. So how do you end a relationship, especially one that has been going on for too long? Most women want to do it in a NICE way, but the fact is no matter how you terminate your connection, he is going to be deeply hurt. And possibly very angry. Breakups, whether it's a long-term marriage or just a brief romance, can be traumatic for both partners, no matter how nicely you do it. So take Paul Simon's advice: "There must be 50 ways to leave your lover." Find one.

When to Commit

Committing to one person is an important decision. You are cutting yourself off from other men who might be superior prospects. So make sure you decide for the right reasons. Don't commit because of sexual attraction or because you are "madly in love." That's not enough to sustain a relationship over the long term.

Avoid the one blunder that probably leads to more unhappy marriages than any other: premature pregnancy. A very high percentage of brides are pregnant on their wedding nights. You're an adult. So prove it by taking simple precautions to plan perhaps the most important responsibility you will undertake in life: becoming a parent.

The Biological Clock

It's easy to watch the years go by as you pursue education and then a high-powered career. Suddenly you discover that you are successful professionally but have a vacancy in your heart. You desperately want a child. So you marry the first half-decent man who comes along who is available.

Be aware that cutting-edge medical technology is now allowing women to bear children into their late 40s and even older. Yes, the risks of miscarriage or birth defects are higher. But allowing desperation to dictate when you marry and bear children is not a wise strategy.

Hold onto your *Must List* and don't compromise to the point where you give up one of more qualities that are essential to you for happiness. You'll just end up raising your child alone. Personal Note: My parents split when I was five. My dad provided financial support, but he wasn't there for me during my childhood. We became good friends much later in my life. I turned out reasonably ok. But who knows how much better life would have been for both me and my mom, if my parents had chosen someone more compatible? There are so many divorces that might have been prevented if only couples chose more wisely!

And They Lived Happily Ever After

So you finally meet someone special. Things are going smoothly. Good communication. Good compatibility. How does a fun relationship become a committed one? How does your bachelor decide to swear off all other women and focus totally on you? The answer is you must give him the most precious gift any human being can give to another—the gift of self-esteem. Psychotherapists will tell you that low self-esteem is at the root of most their clients' problems. We live in a society that does everything in its power to diminish our self-concepts. Parents, then teachers, then friends, employers, coworkers, romantic partners, usually unintentionally reduce our self-worth. If your partner finds that his self-esteem is highest when he is in your presence, you will become indispensable to him. You will be more than a girlfriend, you will be the key to his happiness.

It's a wonder that self-esteem is so scarce in our society, since it is so easy to give. All you have to do is compliment them sincerely and repeatedly. Why sincerely? Most people are so hungry for self-esteem, they will fall for flattery initially. But over time, if you lay it on too thickly, they will start to realize that it's all a sham. They will become suspicious of your past compliments and eventually feel betrayed, They will conclude that your compliments were just a way to seduce them. Then the relationship is as good as over.

Sincere compliments are much harder. You have to observe people closely and notice their talents and good qualities. Compliment them each and every time the occasion arises. And be specific. The more specific the compliment, the more believable and the more convincing it is. Not "you are nice," but "you are so generous in donating your time to tutoring kids at the school down the street." Not "you are a great cook," but "I especially love your beef stroganoff, even better than my mom's."

Making Love Last

As difficult as it is to find the right man and create a successful intimate relationship, the real challenge is make love last. Once the honeymoon stage has expired, strains begin to appear in every romantic partnership. Expecting that things will stay the same is unrealistic. You will be hurt, angry, and disappointed by your partner, as will he. The test is not how do you avoid these problems, but how does your relationship survive despite them?

Good communication has been a constant theme throughout this book. Are both of you able to reveal your feelings? And are both of you able to listen and actually hear the other person, even though their revelations may be quite hurtful?

Open, honest communication is vital. If you or he don't have the requisite skills, your relationship is doomed. Unless you are willing to turn to professional help. Here's where timing is all-important. Don't go into counseling after you have already split apart. As soon as it is evident that you are not communicating your feelings to each other effectively, it's time to call in the expert. The joke among therapists is that none of them are marriage counselors—they are all divorce counselors. Don't let the joke be on you. Ask for help as soon as you realize you need it.

Three more things are critical:

1. Taking responsibility for your own happiness. Expecting him to make you happy is too heavy a burden for any man. That's your job!
2. Asking for what you want. Your partner cannot read your mind. It's your responsibility to be clear about your needs and wants.
3. Accepting no for an answer. Your partner is not obliged to accede to all of your wishes and cater to your every need. If he is willing to really listen to what you need and make a sincere effort to help you in your quest for happiness, you are lucky to have him!

A Final Note

Dating can be hard work. And frustrating. But it can also be a fun adventure. Rather than focusing on all that can go wrong, look at the bright side. If you are committed to meeting someone special, you are going to meet a lot new people, in many new places, doing fun and exciting new activities. Don't let fear prevent you from breaking out of your rut. Don't settle for just surviving. Don't settle for Mr. OK. You know who you want. Go out and find him!

APPENDIX: DONALD TRUMP'S MOST EGREGIOUS LIES

Lies about President Obama and his Administration

1. Trump claims that President Obama wiretapped him. FBI Director James Comey flatly denies this.
2. Trump claims that Obama Founded ISIS. The truth is that ISIS was founded by Abu Masab Al-Zarqawi.
3. Trump claims that the Obama administration actively supported Al Qaeda in Iraq. A total fabrication.
4. Trump claims that the United States unemployment rate was 42 percent under Obama. The truth is that the unemployment rate was only 4.7 percent before Mr. Trump took office.
5. Trump claims that 58% of black youth were unemployed under Obama. The correct figure is 19.2%.
6. Trump claims that his inauguration crowd was larger than Obama's. Photographs of President Obama's first inauguration (in 2009) and that of President Trump in 2017 show that his crowd was much smaller than Obama's.
7. Trump claims that two people were killed during President Obama's Farewell Speech in Chicago. The truth is that no one died during this speech.
8. Trump claims that it was "without precedent" when President Obama visited Saudi Arabia and Cuba and was not greeted at the airport by their leaders. Actually, this has happened many times, to several presidents.
9. Trump claims that millions of people are uninsured because of Obamacare. The opposite is true.
10. Trump claims that Obama tried to delay open enrollment in Obamacare until after the election, because there would be shocking premium increases of 40-60 percent. The truth is that the average increase was 9%. Furthermore, Obama did not have the power to delay the November 1 date because by federal law public notice would have had to be made months earlier.

11. Trump claims that that Obama let 300,000 criminal aliens back into the United States. According to ICE, there were 82,288 criminal aliens in the US. In 2015.

12. Trump claims that President Obama spent $4 million to hide records that would indicate where he was born. The truth is that the Obama for America campaign paid more than $4 million in legal services to a law firm that worked on many issues, not just his birthplace.

13. Trump claims that Obama wanted to let 200,000 refugees in from Syria. The correct number is 185,000 over two years from the entire world, not just Syria.

14. "The Obama administration was actively supporting Al Qaeda in Iraq, the terrorist group that became the Islamic State." Preposterous!

15. Trump claims that Obama's Clean Power Plan "will increase monthly electric bills by double digits without any measurable improvement in climate whatsoever." The Energy Information Administration (non-profit) estimated Obama's plan would result in a 3 percent increase in electricity costs.

16. Trump claims that "The Obama administration, with the support of Hillary Clinton and others, has also damaged our security by restraining our intelligence gathering. And we have just no intelligence gathering information." The truth is that Obama urged Congress to increase counter-terrorism efforts and other measures.

17. "Since President Obama came into office, another 2 million Hispanics have joined the ranks of those in poverty." The truth, according to *The Washington Post*, is that "the number of Hispanics who have been lifted from poverty since 2009 is nearly 1 million, so Trump is off by 3 million net."

18. Trump claims the U.S. murder rate under Obama is the highest it's been in 45 years. The truth is that the rate of homicides and violent crimes is about half the rates when they were highest, during the 1980s and early 1990s.

19. Trump claims that murders have been increasing in Philadelphia under Obama. The truth is that the murder rate has held steady in Philadelphia during the Obama years.

Lies about Hillary Clinton

1. Trump claimed that Hillary Clinton only came out for renegotiating the NAAFTA Agreement in July, 2017 because Trump pushed her to do so. The truth is that she made this pledge in 2008.
2. Trump claimed that Hillary Clinton started the "Birther" Movement. While it is true that some of Clinton's supporters circulated anonymous emails, there's no evidence that Secretary Clinton or her campaign questioned Obama's birth certificate.
3. Trump claimed that Hillary Clinton started the talks that resulted in the shipment of $400 million in cash to Iran at about the same time that four Americans in custody in Iran were freed. The truth is that this $400 million rightfully belonged to Iran, and that talks to give it back to Iran began before she became Secretary of State, and were completed after she left the State Department.
4. Trump claimed that Clinton lacked the stamina to be president. Campaigning for President required enormous stamina from both candidates! Clearly, both Clinton and Trump had the required stamina.
5. Trump claimed that Clinton's emails caused the execution of Shahram Amiri, who defected from Iran. The truth is that Mr. Amiri's defection was reported by the news media, so there was no need to glean this information from Secretary Clinton's emails
6. Trump claimed that Clinton raised $60 million in July, 2016, from just 20 people, Actually, 900,000 made donations to the Clinton campaign in July. The magnitude of this lie is astounding, even for Trump!
7. Trump claimed that Clinton's State Department spent $400 million in aid to build "a massive sweatshop" in Haiti. The facts are that the company pays a minimum wage and provides paid time off and free transportation.
8. Trump claimed that under Clinton illegal immigrants would skip the line and start collecting Social Security benefits. The truth is that people in the U.S. illegally are NOT eligible to collect Social Security benefits.

9. Trump claimed that Clinton "lost" or "misplaced" $6 billion of tax-payer money at the State Department. The truth is that there was missing paperwork for about $6 billion in contracts, but no money was lost, just the paperwork. Most of the $6 billion was spent on projects from the Bush Administration, before Mrs. Clinton became Secretary of State.

10. Trump claimed that The Clinton email scandal was "bigger than Watergate." There is a vast difference between Clinton's scandal and Watergate. Nobody was indicted because of Clinton's emails, whereas 48 people were found guilty of a crime and President Nixon was forced to resign as a result of Watergate.

11. Trump claimed that "She never reveals details about her Immigration Plan. Now that you've heard about Hillary Clinton's plan, about which she has not answered a single question, let me tell you about my plan," said Trump. The truth is that Secretary Clinton repeatedly gave details about her Immigration Plan throughout the campaign.

12. Trump claimed that that "My opponent has no child care plan." Secretary Clinton repeatedly gave details about her child care plan during the campaign.

13. Trump claimed that "Hillary Clinton surged the trade deficit with China 40% as Secretary of State, costing Americans millions of jobs." According to The Washington Post, the trade deficit was 17.5%, not 40%. Furthermore, as Secretary of State, Mrs. Clinton had little power over the trade deficit.

14. Trump claimed that "I would say the co-founder [of ISIS] would be crooked Hillary Clinton." The truth is that Abu Musab Al-Zarqawi was the founder of ISIS.

15. Trump claims that "In her campaign for president, Hillary Clinton has received $100 million in contributions from Wall Street and hedge funds." The correct figure, according to OpenSecrets.org (non-partisan) is $64.3 million.

16. Trump claimed that "Altogether under the Clinton plan, you'd be admitting hundreds of thousands of refugees from the Middle East with no system to prevent radicalization of the children and their children." The true number is 65,000.

17. Trump claimed that Clinton "plans a $1.3 trillion tax hike." The correct figure, according to The Tax Foundation, is "$498 billion over 10 years."

18. Trump claimed that Clinton was responsible for making Iran the "dominant power in the Middle East and on the road to nuclear weapons." The truth, according to *The New York Times*, is that "Tehran gave up 98 percent of its nuclear fuel in the past year, and partly dismantled many of its nuclear facilities, under an accord that had its roots in Mrs. Clinton's time as secretary of state."

19. Trump claimed that "Clinton has the most open border policy..." The truth is that she supported investing billions in securing the border, according to *Politifact*.

20. Trump claimed that "She's pledged to grant mass amnesty." The truth, according to *Politifact*, is that Mrs. Clinton proposed easier paths to citizenship, but has never supported mass amnesty.

21. Trump claimed that "Hillary Clinton's radical judges will virtually abolish the Second Amendment — can't let that happen." The truth, according to *Politifact*, is that Clinton has never advocated repealing or abolishing the Second Amendment.

22. Trump claimed that "Hillary Clinton wants to approve the Trans-Pacific Partnership; that deal will be a disaster for North Carolina, for every state." The truth is that Mrs. Clinton reversed her earlier position when she was Secretary of State and consistently opposed TPP throughout her campaign.

23. Trump claimed that Hillary Clinton "wants to raise taxes on African-American owned businesses to as much as nearly 50 percent more than they're paying now." At no time has Secretary Clinton ever advocated raising anyone's taxes by anything close to 50%.

24. Trump claimed that "Hillary Clinton says she wants to raise taxes on the middle class." According to linguistic experts, the truth is that in the video cited by Mr. Trump, Secretary Clinton said she did NOT want to raise taxes for the middle class.

25. Trump claimed that Clinton wants to shut down family farms" by using "radical regulation," by raising business tax "rates as high as nearly 50 percent" and by taxing "family farms again at death by as much as 45 percent." The truth, according to *Politifact*, is that she

only proposed a 4 percent increase on the wealthy, which would only affect a tiny number of family farms.

26. Trump claimed that "My opponent won't even say the words radical Islamic terror." The truth, according to *Politico*, is that Mrs. Clinton did use the term "radical Islamism" after the Orlando massacre.

27. Trump claimed that under Clinton's plan "illegal immigrants convicted of committing crimes get to stay." The truth, according to *USA Today*, is that Mrs. Clinton proposed that people with less than three misdemeanors could stay in the U.S. She never supported allowing violent or dangerous criminals to stay.

28. Trump claimed that Clinton "has spent her entire life making money for special interests — and I will tell you, she has made plenty of money for them, and she has been taking plenty of money out for herself." This is a total fabrication. According to *The New York Times*, Mrs. Clinton's career has primarily been in government service. She did work for the non-profit Children's Defense Fund. Is this the "special interest" Mr. Trump finds offensive? Clinton also defended intellectual property.

29. Trump claimed that Clinton is "proposing to print instant work permits for millions of illegal immigrants to come in and take everybody's jobs, including low-income African-Americans." The truth, according to *Politifact*, is that Clinton proposed giving green cards to students who were already in the U.S. legally, many of whom had skills that are not widely available among low-income Americans.

30. Trump claimed that "She will appoint justices that will make our country Venezuela." This is not only a lie, it is total nonsense.

31. Trump claimed that Clinton's "plan would tax many small businesses by almost 50 percent." The truth, according to *The Washington Post*, is that this would only apply to "less than 2 percent of individuals that report at least half of their income from business. About 90 percent of taxpayers with business income make under $200,000, and thus would not be affected by the individual tax increases under Clinton's plan."

32. Trump claimed that "For the amount of money Hillary Clinton would like to spend on refugees, we could rebuild every inner city in America." The truth is that It would cost hundreds of billions

of dollars to rebuild our inner cities. Mrs. Clinton never advocated spending that amount on refugees. President Obama proposed only $2.2 billion.

33. Trump claimed that Clinton "is a bigot. She is selling [African-Americans] down the tubes because she's not doing anything for those communities. She talks a good game. But she doesn't do anything." This is a typical Trump lie, accusing someone of a fault that he may have himself. Nobody who is objective thinks that Clinton is a bigot. To the contrary, she had very strong support from the black community throughout her primary and general election campaign. On the other hand, Mr. Trump's company was sued by the federal government for housing discrimination against African-Americans.

34. Trump claimed that "NAFTA, which her husband signed, is a very, very big reason [for economic problems in upstate New York]." According to *The Washington Post*, NAFTA was both negotiated and signed by President Bush.

35. Trump interrupted Clinton during one presidential debate, saying "Wrong," when Clinton said about Trump, "You've said you'd negotiate down the national debt." Yet Trump did say he'd negotiate down the national debt during a debate during the Republican Primary, according to *CNN*.

Miscellaneous Lies

1. Trump charged that Mexico exports its murderers and rapists illegally across the American border. Many studies show that undocumented immigrants do not commit crimes at a higher rate than American citizens.

2. Trump claimed that scores of recent migrants were charged with terrorism. Actually there only were 30 naturalized American citizens charged with terrorism, and most of them came to the U.S. before 9/11.

3. Trump claimed that Crime is "through the roof," particularly in California, because of illegal immigration. The truth is that violent

crimes have steadily declined for more than a decade in California and around the U.S.

4. Trump claimed that Judge Gonzalo Curiel had an "inherent conflict of interest" in the Trump University fraud case, because he is Mexican. This scurrilous attack is not just a lie, it is a racist lie. Even fellow Republican Speaker of the House Paul Ryan labeled this statement by Trump as the "textbook definition of racism."

5. Trump claimed he started Trump University as a charitable endeavor. Apparently Trump's charity was himself, since he received $5 million from the "University." No donations were ever made to charitable organizations.

6. Trump claimed that he never spoke to the Florida Attorney General before making donations to her. She was investigating fraud claims against Trump University, which she dropped after she received the donations.

7. Trump claims he doesn't get sued a lot, because he rarely settles. The truth is that he settles many, many lawsuits.

8. Trump claimed that "Thousands and thousands" of Muslims in New Jersey cheered when the Twin Towers collapsed on September 11. While we all watched TV coverage of Muslims cheering the collapse, they were all Palestinians abroad. There is no evidence of Muslims in New Jersey cheering on 9/11.

9. Trump claimed on multiple occasions that he had opposed the Iraq War before it started. The truth is that Trump supported the Iraq War originally (it's all on tape) and opposed it later, when it became unpopular.

10. Trump said admiringly that Saddam Hussein was good at killing terrorists. The truth is that rather than kill them, Hussein provided heavy support to terrorist organizations. He was very good at killing his own people, however, especially with poison gas.

11. Trump claimed he raised six million dollars for veterans. Wrong by several millions.

12. Trump claimed he received awards on the environment. There is no evidence that he even received one such award.

13. Trump claimed he would save $300 billion per year by allowing Medicare to negotiate directly with drug companies. The

prescription drug portion of Medicare only costs $78 billion a year, and it's absurd for him to say that he could totally eliminate that expense. The only way to do that would be for Medicare to stop providing any prescription drugs!

14. Trump claimed that between three million and five million illegal votes cost him to lose the popular vote in the 2016 election. There is no evidence whatsoever for this preposterous claim.

15. Trump claimed that 28,000 jobs would be created by the Keystone Pipeline. The truth is that many fewer jobs would be created, and most of them would be one-time jobs during the construction of the pipeline, with only a few thousand being permanent.

16. Trump claimed he won in the Electoral College by a huge margin. It was actually one of the smaller margins in American history.

17. Trump claimed all the polls said he won the Second Presidential Debate with Hillary Clinton. The truth is that every scientific poll showed that Clinton won the debate. Many of the polls showed she won by a wide margin.

18. Trump claimed that airports are not allowed to profile potential terrorists. Since 9/11 security personnel at airports have had this option.

19. Trump first claimed he voted for George Bush, then on another occasion said he didn't "vote for that dimwit." One of these statements is obviously a lie.

20. Trump claimed he built his business empire "with a small loan from my father." Actually, Trump inherited about $40 million from his father. He also received numerous loans and loan guarantees from his father. He also had the advantage of his dad's business and political connections. Fred Trump also partially bailed him out when his Atlantic City casinos went bankrupt.

21. Trump promised he would provide medical care for all. All except the 24 million who would have lost their medical care if TrumpCare had passed Congress!

22. Trump promised his 2,000 mile border wall would cost only $8 billion. The true figure is a low estimate of $25 billion, to higher estimates of over $70 billion.

23. Trump claimed there is "nothing to learn" from releasing his tax returns. Actually, there is much that might be learned from them. For example, that he has business dealings abroad, including with Russia, that might influence his foreign policy. Or that he isn't as rich as he claims.

24. Trump claimed that Governor John Kasich (one of Trump's opponents in the Republican Primary) helped Lehman Brothers "destroy the world economy." Kasich was one of 700 managing directors at Lehman, and played no part in the risky loans that led to financial disaster.

25. Trump claimed that no negative ads were run against Governor Kasich. Actually Trump and other candidates ran many ads attacking Kasich.

26. Trump claimed that Governor Scott Walker (another of Trump's opponents) was responsible for Wisconsin going from a $1 billion surplus to a $2.2 billion deficit. Trump claimed *Time* magazine as his source. Both were lies.

27. Trump claimed he did not mock a disabled reporter, despite TV footage that we have all seen again and again. Who are we going to believe, Trump, or our "lyin' eyes?"

28. Trump claims that Megyn Kelly of *Fox News* lied when she said he used slurs against women. All of these slurs have been documented.

29. Trump claimed that ISIS "is making a fortune now" on oil in Libya. ISIS has captured zero oil fields in Libya.

30. Trump claimed that his tax plan "would cost me a fortune." The opposite is true. Trump would save a bundle if his plan was ever enacted.

31. Trump claimed that We are "a nation of jobless Americans," because 92 million do not have a job. The truth is that 93% of these "jobless Americans" choose not to enter the workforce.

32. Putin called Trump "a genius." Actually the President of Russia used a term that can be translated as "colorful, flamboyant," or "lively."

33. Trump claimed that "They [the 9/11 hijackers] put their families on airplanes a couple of days before, sent them back to Saudi Arabia, for the most part."

34. Trump denied that he had ever said that it might be good for Japan to acquire nuclear weapons, despite videotape to the contrary.
35. Trump claimed that he would eliminate America's 19 Trillion Dollar Debt in eight years. This is mathematically impossible. Even if he eliminated all government function, 16 Trillion Dollars of debt would still remain.
36. Trump claimed that "I have nothing to do with Russia." This contradicts Trump's own son, Donald Trump, Jr., who claims major business interests in Russia for Trump's companies.
37. Trump claimed that veterans "are treated worse" than illegal immigrants. The facts are that veterans receive many benefits and rights that the undocumented do not share.

Some may defend President Trump by arguing that the lies above were not intentional, that he merely exaggerates. In that case, at least he is guilty of a reckless disregard for the truth.

Insinuations

Often Trumps insinuates a falsehood, without actually lying. For example, that

1. President Obama was not born in the United States. Trump later recanted and admitted that Obama was born in the U.S., after falsely implying for years that Obama was born abroad.
2. President Obama may have caused a murder: "How amazing, the State Health Director who verified copies of Obama's "birth certificate" died in plane crash today. All others live."
3. There is something "very fishy" about the death of Hillary and Bill Clinton's close friend and White House Deputy Counsel Vincent W. Foster. Trump also called theories of foul play "very serious." Five probes have failed to find any evidence to support this outrageous hypothesis.
4. Linking Ted Cruz's father with the Kennedy Assassination. There is no evidence for this.

5. Vaccines may cause Autism. There is no scientific evidence backing up this up.
6. Secretary Clinton accepted jewelry from the leaders of Brunei valued at $58,000. Mr. Trump implied that she kept it for her personal use. However, according to the *New York Times*, she may have accepted this gift but was required to transfer it to the federal government.
7. "Hillary Clinton is raising your taxes, it's a very substantial tax increase." Mrs. Clinton only wanted to increase taxes on households over $250,000 in income, which is a small percentage of the country's population. So at best, Mr. Trump's statement was only slightly true and very misleading.

Sources: These lies (and hundreds more!) are documented by the *Washington Post's Fact Checker* (non-partisan) and BombasticLiar.com.

And the Lies Continue...

Since his inauguration on January 20, 2017, "Trump achieved something remarkable," according to *The New York Times* (June 23, 2017). "He said something untrue, in public, every day for the first 40 days of his presidency. The streak didn't end until March 1." The article goes on to chronicle 98 Trump lies since he assumed the office of President, including these whoppers:

1. His Inauguration crowd was much larger than Obama's (it was much smaller).
2. 3-5 million illegal votes cost him the popular vote (there is no evidence of this)
3. He didn't want to invade Iraq during in 2003 (there is a radio interview tape that proves he supported the invasion)
4. The New York Times apologized for its poor reporting of the presidential campaign (never happened)
5. The U.S. murder rate is the highest it has been in 47 years (the murder rate was actually higher during the 1980s and 1990s)

6. His electoral vote total was the highest since Reagan (George Bush senior, Bill Clinton, and Barack Obama all had more electoral votes)
7. He was responsible for Walmart creating 10,000 more jobs (these jobs were announced three months before he became president)
8. Obamacare covers very few people (it covers 20 million)
9. NATO is obsolete because it does not fight terrorism (NATO has fought terrorism since the 1980s)
10. Half of Tennessee had no health insurance company in its marketplace (all of Tennessee has at least one company from which to choose)
11. There was no vetting and no documentation for refugees entering the U.S. during the Obama Administration (there was two years of vetting and documentation)
12. The Environmental Protection Agency (EPA) caused the loss of hundreds of thousands of jobs during the Obama Administration (no evidence of this)
13. "122 vicious prisoners" were released from Guantanamo under President Obama (113 of the 122 were released by President George W. Bush)
14. The recapture of Mosul from ISIS was only supposed to take a week (the U.S. Military predicted it would take months)
15. Democrats were blocking the healthcare for miners bill.(the bill was introduced by a Democrat and was mainly co-sponsored by Democrats)
16. The U.S. had a $17 billion trade deficit with Canada (actually there was an $8.1 billion trade SURPLUS in 2016.)
17. The Paris Climate Change Agreement allows India and China to build hundreds of coal plants (the agreement makes no such allowance)
18. Trump claimed he caused Lockheed to cut the cost of its planes (these cuts were planned before the election)
19. No one except reporters cares that Trump withholds his tax returns (the polls show a majority of Americans want him to release the returns)

www.ingramcontent.com/pod-product-compliance
Lightning Source LLC
Chambersburg PA
CBHW071638050426
42443CB00026B/720